P9-CMF-805

Also by Andrew Tully

A Race of Rebels
Treasury Agent
Era of Elegance

When They Burned
the
White House

by

Andrew Tully

Drawings by Milton Glaser

SIMON AND SCHUSTER • NEW YORK • 1961

E
356
W3
T8

All rights reserved
including the right of reproduction
in whole or in part in any form
Copyright © 1961 by Andrew Tully
Published by Simon and Schuster, Inc.
Rockefeller Center, 630 Fifth Avenue
New York 20, N.Y.

First Printing

Library of Congress Catalog Card Number: 61–7009
Manufactured in the United States of America
Printed by Halliday Lithograph Corp.
Bound by American Book–Stratford Press, Inc.

42732

FERNALD LIBRARY
COLBY JUNIOR COLLEGE
NEW LONDON, N.H. 03257

For Martha, Liz, Sheila,
Andrew and Mark
With Love

ACKNOWLEDGMENTS

Many people helped, directly or indirectly, knowingly or unknowingly, in the writing of this book about one of America's darkest hours. Because so little had been written previously about the burning of Washington during the War of 1812, the research involved was extensive, and this required call after call upon the services and good nature of many selfless public servants devoted to the unearthing and dissemination of historical information.

The author owes a special debt to Mrs. Della Wilson, who

7

assisted in research and typing and in many other chores outside the wonted sphere of the casual assistant.

Special and interested help also was given without stint by the staffs at the Library of Congress, the District of Columbia Library, the Smithsonian Institution, the Columbia Historical Society, the office of the Architect of the Capitol, the White House and the Lincoln Museum. From time to time the author found assistance, too, among the members of the staff of Senator Hubert Humphrey of Minnesota and from various officials of the Department of Defense.

Finally, whatever worth there may be in this book was enhanced by the expert efforts of Robert Gottlieb, managing editor of Simon and Schuster, Inc., who kept the author from stumbling too much and is not responsible for whatever deficiencies may have been caused by the author's literary idiosyncrasies.

ANDREW TULLY

Washington, D.C.
September 1, 1960

8

CONTENTS

Acknowledgments   7

Foreword   11

I   Beachhead   15

II   "The British Are Coming"   27

III   Defenders of the Capital   41

IV   Rally to the Cause   52

V   Redcoats on the March   67

• CONTENTS •

VI   *Compromise City*   76

VII   *Dolly's Palace*   89

VIII   *Chaos by the Campfires*   105

IX   *Rabble on the Field*   116

X   *"The Rockets' Red Glare"*   130

XI   *Flight from Washington*   144

XII   *"Burn It, Sir!"*   155

XIII   *A Castle in Flames*   165

XIV   *"Use Your Own Soap"*   179

XV   *Retreat—and Return*   192

XVI   *"Is the Flag Still There?"*   208

XVII   *The Phoenix Rises Again*   216

XVIII   *"Is It Peace?"*   230

FOREWORD

One of the difficulties encountered in writing any book of this kind is the necessity for choosing between two or more sources which offer contradictory evidence. This was especially true in seeking out intelligence on the burning of Washington because the records are so scanty and incomplete. Sometimes, too, it seemed as if everybody with a pen and a piece of paper had a different version of what happened.

There was only one thing to do, and that was to favor the version which was in the majority—that is, to accept that evi-

dence which was submitted by a preponderance of the sources consulted.

For instance, there is some disagreement as to whether Admiral Cockburn actually stood up in the Capitol and asked a vote on whether "this harbor of Yankee democracy be burned." But the incident was reported too often to be ignored or to split hairs over its probable accuracy. Moreover, it sounded like something Cockburn would say; it had the Cockburn flavor.

There are documents, too, which dispute the report that when the British entered the White House they found a banquet prepared for President Madison's expected supper guests. But history is most convincing on this point; there is the note Mrs. Jones, wife of the Secretary of the Navy, wrote Dolly Madison expressing her regrets she would not be able to be present at the feast.

Some sources claim that Joseph Gales, editor of the National Intelligencer, *was visiting kinfolk during the burning of Washington. But more sources—including the estimable and painstaking Glenn Tucker—place him on the battlefield as the first war correspondent in the weanling nation's history. So that is where he is in this book.*

Finally, there is the matter of the spelling of Mrs. Madison's first name. Much has been made of the fact that she signed it Dolley. *She did. But there are many documents also which show her signing it without the e—that is,* Dolly. *The author stuck with* Dolly *for this reason and because that spelling is more acceptable today.*

Here and there, dialogue and the gestures of characters have been invented. That is unavoidable in any attempt to give life to what are sometimes the bare bones of a historical incident.

But if an author lives with his characters for any decent length of time, he gets to know them and to acquire an idea of how they would speak and act in a given situation.

However, no liberties have been taken with historical facts as set down by sources both respected and in the majority. Within the limitations of the author, this is presented as an accurate and historically authentic story of the burning of Washington during the strange War of 1812.

ANDREW TULLY

[I]

Beachhead

IN THE MOIST DAWN of August 19, 1814, Lieutenant George Robert Gleig of His Majesty's 85th Light Infantry Regiment paced the deck of a ship-of-war as its captain prepared to drop anchor in the Patuxent River, eight miles below the little town of Benedict in the state of Maryland.

The American shore looked green and fresh even in the early heat which had set the river shimmering. After the long voyage from Spain via Bermuda, Gleig was anxious to set foot on dry land. He thought of fresh eggs, milk and vegetables, and water free of crawling things, and was determined to be in one of the first small boats to start up the river transporting the troops to land. But his eagerness betrayed him; he found himself with sixty men and a brother officer suddenly jammed into an un-wieldy, broad-nosed punt with only two oarmen.

"Damme," Gleig told the other officer, "we'll be on this blasted river all day."

Swiftly, Gleig calculated the boat's progress; he decided it was moving upstream at a miserly half-mile per hour.

"Why, we may as well jump in and swim," said Gleig. "It will take us sixteen hours to reach Benedict. And in this broil-ing American sun."

Frantically, the two officers sought assistance from their fellows passing them in the speedier barges. "Heave us a line!" they yelled. "Give us a tow!"

Their comrades seemed to think it was funny. Hoots and vulgar suggestions greeted them. "We'll stop and pick you up on the way back," one officer shouted.

And another yelled, "Why don't you hire a blinking coach-and-four!"

The impromptu vaudeville continued for more than an hour, while Gleig sweated and fumed and the men fidgeted and cursed the Royal Navy. It wasn't until Gleig spotted a midship-man he had known in London that the punt was rescued. The midshipman acknowledged his obligation to friendship and threw them a line. Thereafter, they made good way up the river, although it was almost noon when Gleig's boat touched shore at Benedict.

Gleig, an articulate and perceptive subaltern, may have sensed the history that hung over that steaming day. For he was a member of a punitive force dispatched to bring the war home to those raffish renegade Britons known as Americans. The expedition's plans were still flexible—that is, it was prepared to strike wherever circumstances dictated—but within a few days this British force would be setting the torch to the capital city of Washington, thirty-eight miles away.

Despite Great Britain's official sneers at its quondam colonists, this was an elite force scrambling ashore at Benedict. It consisted of 5,123 men, composing four line regiments and a detachment of Marines, and almost all were hard-eyed veterans of the recent Peninsula campaign against Napoleon. Of this army, the 4th (King's Own) and the 44th line regiments boasted brilliant records. On the first day of the American Revolution, the 4th had suffered forty-four casualties in protecting the British detachment which was forced back from Concord Bridge to Boston. Two months later, the 4th swarmed over the American trenches at Bunker Hill. The 44th had fought in the French and Indian War, and had passed in review with Washington's Virginians at Fort Duquesne. Both had distinguished themselves in the attack that broke the French at Talavera, causing Wellington to remark that "I could have done anything with that army." Compared to these regiments, Gleig's 85th was a parvenu, having been formed in 1793, but in the same year it was mentioned several times in the Peninsula dispatches.

For reasons of strategy, the British command was split. Leading the troops was General Robert Ross, an Irish gentleman, graduate of Dublin's Trinity College, and one of the major heroes of Wellington's victory over the Corsican. He was a man with a calm air of assurance: an urbane individual and a strict disciplinarian capable of drilling troops ten hours a day in the quiet garrison at Malta. The British army commander had come to the Chesapeake directly from the Peninsula campaign, about which Wellington had commented: "General Ross's brigade distinguished themselves beyond all former precedent."

Those ships earmarked from Admiral Sir Alexander Cochrane's fleet for the invasion were under the command of Admiral Sir George Cockburn, able, brave and militarily profound, but a noisy swaggerer whose coarseness was infamous even for that seafaring day. Cockburn had spent nearly two years as a commander in the Chesapeake blockade in which he had raided and pillaged the cities and towns with the unthinking cruelty of a Mongol chieftain. American estimates calculated that Cockburn destroyed $1,500,000 worth of tobacco during the spring and summer of 1814. At Havre de Grace, Cockburn's men burned or destroyed forty of the sixty houses, two taverns, ten stables, a blacksmith shop, a sawmill, a bridge, several ferryboats and a couple of stages. Later, when the British had moved on the village of Hampton, on the north shore of the James River, Cockburn promised his men "booty and beauty," and they got both. Scores of women were raped, some of them by renegade Negro slaves who had been encouraged by the invaders to turn on their masters. A man named Kirby, who had been lying at the point of death for six weeks, was murdered in his bed; his wife took a bullet in the hip.

Cockburn shared in the loot, accepting two incongruous prizes at Havre de Grace. One was a carriage which had cost one thousand dollars, and the other was a sofa.

"I'll use the carriage," said Cockburn, "to ride in triumph about the Yankee towns we capture."

The admiral enjoyed tossing off such remarks, which he regarded as the height of humor, and this one, like so many others, wound up in one of Cockburn's letters to the profligate Prince Regent. That Royal Highness considered the war with America almost as side-splitting as the imbecilic antics of the aging King George III, in whose name the Prince had taken over the reins of Empire.

Cockburn and Ross were as different in military method as they were in bearing and in discipline, and when they first went ashore, near the mouth of the Potomac, they could not agree as to the proper strategy. Ross, a practical early-day intellectual, wanted to mount an attack on Baltimore. He pointed out its great commercial importance as the third largest city in the United States and one of the principal shipping centers of the fledgling nation. Moreover, it was the home port of many of the American privateersmen which had been harrying British merchantmen for nearly two years.

But Cockburn held out for flexibility, for a plan that would keep the Americans off balance, and Ross finally agreed to it. The major portion of the fleet was to enter the Patuxent and the army was to debark and take a position from which it could strike at either Baltimore or Washington, or perhaps Annapolis. This, it was believed, would cause the Americans to divide their available forces so as to furnish protection for all three cities.

Meanwhile, a small flotilla under Captain James A. Gordon, commander of the frigate *Seahorse*, would sail up the Potomac, destroy Fort Washington, twelve miles below the capital, and lay siege to Alexandria. Then it would lie ready to co-operate with Ross if the general decided to attack Washington.

Ross wished he had more men. He knew he would have to leave a force at Benedict to protect the point where his troops undoubtedly would have to re-embark after accomplishing their business ashore. An additional detachment would have to be stationed along the route to guard a possible retreat and to maintain his supply line. But it couldn't be helped, and, anyway, he had the quality which counted so much in an expedition of this kind.

Cockburn was to take his Marines up the river in tenders while Ross marched along the roadway so that the two could act together if they met opposition from the little American flotilla of tiny gunboats commanded by a gruff and irascible commodore named Joshua Barney. Barney's fleet had given Cockburn much trouble during the Chesapeake campaign and now the doughty commodore waited with sixteen boats at Pig Point, fifteen miles up the Patuxent.

Cockburn was exultant. "By God," he told Ross, "at last I'm going to lay my hands on that Barney. I'll make him pay for his bloody impudence."

Ross was not so sanguine. He pointed out that the only horse in the expeditionary force was his own mount, and that he was most deficient in artillery. There were plenty of guns with the fleet, but since seamen would have to drag them on the march, Ross could take with him only two three-pounders and one six-pounder.

The force also had a new and spectacular weapon which fascinated the men but left Ross unimpressed. This was the Congreve rocket, an invention of Sir William Congreve, a

British artillery officer, who had first used it during Admiral Nelson's bombardment of Copenhagen. It was a twelve-pound sheet-iron tube with a projectile at the head that exploded like an artillery shell.

Cockburn had first fired the rocket on American soil during his bombardment and sacking of Havre de Grace the summer before. But although the rocket's red glare frightened some women and children, it was found ineffective as a weapon, since it had force only at short range and was difficult to aim with any precision. Ross could only hope that at least its hideous novelty might have a damaging psychological effect on the American defenders, although this thought afforded little consolation.

While Ross and Cockburn pondered problems of military strategy, Lieutenant George Robert Gleig's concern was directed toward his new surroundings in the strange, deserted town of Benedict. It had been abandoned by its inhabitants when the news had come that the monster Cockburn was among the invading force.

The 85th Light Infantry Regiment bivouacked on a grassy slope just under the ridge of a low hill, and while the men were building cooking fires and getting out provisions, Gleig and some fellow-officers strolled about the town, curious to see how the Americans lived. They found most of the homes simple, consisting of few rooms and dominated by a large combination kitchen-living room with big fireplace. Each house had an attached dairy stocked with cheeses and crocks of milk whose sides glistened with moisture. To deter the men from looting, the word had been passed that the Americans had poisoned their food supplies, but Gleig's appetite was not to be deterred by such a ruse. He drank more than a quart of the first milk he had seen in months, and helped himself to some cheese.

Another member of the British force—a private soldier—was getting his midday dinner in gayer company, with a romantic bonus thrown in. The soldier, identified in the records only as "Stubbs," sneaked away from the bivouac in the middle of the confusion of the disembarkation and went rustling about the outskirts of Benedict to investigate the looting possibilities.

He was about to break into a small cottage, about a mile from the camp, when he heard a lilting—and unmistakably feminine—voice behind him. "Please wait. Please wait," the voice was saying.

The soldier whirled and found himself confronted by a bucolic lass with long black hair and ample bosom poorly concealed by an off-the-shoulder smock.

"I'll open the door for you," she told Stubbs, and gave him a minxish smile. Stubbs examined her swiftly and found her face was clear and fairly clean. And she smelled of that barnyard smell composed largely of fresh milk. He grabbed her arm.

"Open the door," he told her, "and then in with you, my little bawd."

They went into the cottage and Stubbs fastened the door. Then he checked the two rooms lest a male be concealed about the place. Finding the cottage empty, he asked the girl, "What have you to eat?"

Her face brightened. "Oh, ham and some cheeses and some milk," she told him.

"Then lay it out on the table," Stubbs ordered.

22

The two of them sat at the table while Stubbs wolfed the country food and the girl nibbled daintily on a cheese. When Stubbs had eaten his fill, she rose and crooked an index finger at the British soldier. Stubbs emerged from the cottage an hour later, his stomach and his maleness satisfied, carrying a ham and a wheel of cheese as souvenirs.

General Ross's men could well take advantage of these luxuries of war, because it was evident they would only be temporary and that the march to come would be a hard one. Not only were there no horses for the officers, but there were no pack mules to carry supplies, and the tents that had sheltered the men in Europe had been left on the ships.

Each officer, like the soldiers, carried his equipment and provisions on his back. Gleig's burden included the usual saber, sash, belt, two pistols and a telescope. Strapped across his shoulders was a heavy cloak, and slung over his left shoulder was a black leather haversack containing a spare shirt, a pair of stockings, toilet gear, a foraging cap, three pounds of boiled pork and two and a half pounds of sea biscuit. A horn filled with purser's rum hung from his neck in front, and a wooden water keg was strapped to his back.

Some of the British officers grumbled at this; they felt it beneath the dignity of the Empire to campaign without the conveniences of the officer class.

"We're marching like bloody American officers," a comrade muttered to Gleig. "An officer should travel like a gentleman."

It wasn't quite that bad, of course. The officers still had their batmen, and Gleig's Portuguese boy was watching a potful of potatoes and green vegetables which he had liberated from one of the kitchen gardens in the village. Gleig ate the stew with generous side helpings from his loot of cheese.

Lieutenant Gleig, soldier Stubbs, and the other troops who had landed early would live thus off the fat of Benedict's land for two days, since it took that long for Ross to debark his entire force. But they were busy days, too, because Ross feared harassment from small Yankee forces striking from the surrounding forests, and not only surrounded his camp with pickets but kept patrols constantly on the move against possible guerrillas.

It was on one of these patrols that an officer of the 4th Regiment became separated from his men and, wandering down a road cut through the woods about two miles from Benedict, arrived at a large farmhouse. Assuming it was deserted, he barged in and found himself an unexpected guest of four large Yankee males.

He should have been the first British prisoner of the campaign, but despite their size and their four-to-one advantage, these Americans were typical of a citizenry which had been terror-stricken by the Ross-Cockburn invasion. All four threw up their hands in surrender, and the British officer recovered from his surprise fast enough to hold them in that pose with his two pistols while he mustered his thoughts.

One of the Yanks rescued him from the necessity of forming a plan for his own escape. "Don't call in your men," he pleaded. "We're not soldiers. We're poor farmers. Please let us go. We won't do any harm."

Coolly now, the Britisher took command. He ordered one of the men to pass him a freshly dressed chicken lying on the kitchen table, and paid for it with a new shilling.

"Now," he told them, "my men and I are merely foraging for provisions. I'm convinced you are not soldiers, and so we won't harm you. But you had best stay inside the house the rest of the afternoon or you may get in trouble with another patrol." Then he departed, the fowl under his arm, and made his way safely back to the bivouac.

It was, of course, a cliché in the British Army that all Americans were cowards, and the four burly Yankees seemed to prove the point. Meanwhile, another patrol discovered that some of the defenders of the Patuxent were equally obliging.

There had been reports that a small band of American riflemen had spent the night in a wooded section to the south of Benedict. A Lieutenant Smythe took a patrol out to try to find this sample of the enemy. Shortly, the British soldiers came on signs of a campfire indicating the Americans had quit the site only recently.

Lieutenant Smythe walked on carefully, slightly in advance of his men. After going a thousand yards or so, he thought he saw a silvery glint through the trees. Quickly, he sent files of soldiers in several different directions so as to surround the spot. Then, moving forward, he saw two Yankees, dressed in somber black coats and armed with muskets and bayonets, lolling under a tree.

The two Americans saw Smythe almost as soon as he saw them and took to their heels. But they were hemmed in, and after going a few hundred yards they stopped and waited for Smythe and his men to catch up with them.

As Smythe strode up, he was startled to hear one of the men tell the other: "Stop, John, till the gentlemen pass."

Smythe burst into laughter. "You are right, sir," he told

them. "We *are* gentlemen, but we are also British soldiers and you are our prisoners."

A look of incredulity came over the face of the soldier addressed as John. "But we're not soldiers," he said. "We're just plain folk, out after squirrels."

"Oh," said Smythe, "and I presume your bayonets are to charge the squirrels after you've shot them. We'll take those rifles, sirs, and you will come with us."

The invaders from perfidious Albion could not have known it at the time, but these two incidents were a portent of what was to come as the British force marched up the Patuxent. For the United States of America, as represented by its military defenders of the capital city, was unready and often unwilling to join battle with the enemy. General Ross, with his fetish for alert pickets and his fear of ambuscades on the march, was about to move against a population very nearly demoralized by fear.

[II]

"The British Are Coming"

TWENTY-FOUR HOURS before Lieutenant Gleig and his fellows debarked at Benedict, "Copenhagen" Jackson was making his way north toward the rectangular Capitol building. A carpenter whose hours were his own, Jackson was embarked on a day's hunting, planning to pass through the town of Bladensburg and seek deer in the heavy woods to the northwest of that port.

Humming a tune, Jackson strode happily through the weeds

and light brush that covered the Capitol grounds and gave an approving eye to the two blocks of Virginia sandstone which were the House and Senate wings of what some people called the "House of Legislature." The lines of the building were clean and simple, but Jackson wished the powers responsible would rattle their hocks and get started on the dome which would surmount the center of the building, between the two wings.

Jackson turned to the west and was about to plunge into a field whose browning grasses stood waist-high when there was a whirring sound ahead. He brought his hunting musket up to his shoulder for a quick aim, but he was too late. The covey of pheasants had zoomed out of range.

Chagrined, Jackson continued on his way. He spent four hours in the woods but that covey of pheasants at the Capitol was the last sign he saw of game. And when he trudged back to Washington in mid-afternoon on that sultry Thursday— August 18, 1814—his wife and friends surrounded him to impart the ominous news. The British were coming.

The news had come officially that morning, only an hour after Jackson had set out for deer. It was brought by a courier on a foam-specked horse, who raced up Pennsylvania Avenue, cloaking the loafers under Thomas Jefferson's poplars with clouds of dust. At the War Department, the courier identified himself as a member of the detachment from the army's observatory station at Point Lookout, where the Potomac enters the Chesapeake.

The British fleet, he informed the bureaucratic brass, had been seen entering the Patuxent, obviously making for anchorage near the town of Benedict. Large bodies of troops seen on the ships indicated a major land movement.

Nobody tried to keep the news a secret. Within an hour, most of Washington was trembling under its portent. It interrupted the graceless patrons of a "Bathe House" on the avenue where the proprietor offered "Warm, Temperate and Cold Baths for the Use of the Citizenry. Terms, Three Warm and Four Cold Baths for 100 Cents." Crowds gathered for news bulletins at the office of the *National Intelligencer* at Sixth Street and the avenue. In Georgetown, Mrs. Samuel Harrison Smith, wife of the noted banker and first Commissioner of the Revenue of the Treasury Department, began collecting silver and linen for removal to a farm outside the city.

By the time Copenhagen Jackson returned home, the more excitable of the capital's 8,000 inhabitants already had begun their exodus into the countryside. Whole families had taken the road to Montgomery Courthouse in Maryland, later to be renamed Rockville, their movable possessions bundled into carriages or pulled in hand-drawn wagons, or pushed in wheelbarrows. The streets were crowded with people, who kicked up a constant haze of reddish dust.

Clerks in the Federal Departments already were stowing records and documents of the moment into boxes and trunks for removal elsewhere. Inside the banks, everybody lent a hand to the business of moving the money into wagons drawn up at their doors to carry the shipments to Hagerstown, Maryland.

Copenhagen Jackson decided that he would stay in Washington. "It's just a lot of bloody Englishmen," he told his wife. And when she countered with tales of Cockburn's depredations in the Chesapeake, he told her to be silent.

"Do just stay indoors," Copenhagen advised her sharply.

"You're not a tart to hang about in the streets and stare at the redcoats."

Outside the office of the *National Intelligencer,* some in the crowd muttered against its editor, Joe Gales, a man of careless erudition who long had been a semi-official spokesman for President Madison. For months now Gales had been scoffing at reports that a British invasion was in the offing; he apparently felt that by allaying the fears of the populace he was protecting his President.

Although Admiral Cockburn himself had bellowed that his hands itched to get at Gales's throat, the mutterers outside his office accused him of serving "foreign interests." Particularly, they linked Gales with the absurd rumors that Madison had been in league with Napoleon and had planned to cede a piece of American territory to the Corsican in exchange for military help against Albion.

Gales did not show up outside, considering it beneath his dignity to bicker with the rabble.

Gales had a right to his dignity, for he was a man of distinction among the British as well as among the residents of the dusty capital. Next to Madison, he probably was the American most hated by the invaders—mostly because of an accident of birth.

The editor had been born in Sheffield, where his father published the Sheffield *Register,* and thus he was considered by the English to be subject to British law. Moreover, father and son had fled to America as political refugees in 1795. They had gone first to North Carolina, where the father published the Raleigh *Register.* Young Joe Gales had come to Washington in 1810, when he bought the *Intelligencer* from Samuel Harrison Smith, and two years later he took on as a partner his brother-in-law, William W. Seaton.

As reporter as well as editor, it was Gales who caused the United States Senate to establish its first press gallery. This was a chair on the front rostrum, alongside the seat occupied by the then Vice President, George Clinton. Gales sat there almost every day, swapping snuff boxes with Clinton.

Now Gales had on his hands a story he had never believed would occur—a British attack on Washington. That day, in his ink-splotched newspapers, he gave a vivid description of the atmosphere in the capital city during the first few hours of the alarm. It was a bustling scene that Gales observed.

The dandies were out, of course, to enjoy the excitement. They moved about in a determined stroll, dudish in the new long pantaloons, tail coats with high, rolling collars, and tall hats of light shades. Older and more sober men, not yet won over to the French style in this period of transition for male haberdashery, went their way in their breeches and long stockings, some with powder on their hair.

The respectable women either kept to their homes to pack or were already struggling along the streets with husbands and families, all carrying or pulling their possessions to safety. But the fancy girls, like the dandies, saw fun in the turmoil. Along Pennsylvania Avenue and in the dusty side streets bordered by wooden shacks, they turned out in their long, flowing evening dresses with their provocative off-the-shoulder bodices.

Although they all had a flamboyant air, most of these easy-mannered girls looked better in their clothes than the great ladies of the town. The ugly turbans of the time seemed chic on their heads and they wore their cashmere shawls with grace.

Their rounded figures showed to good advantage in their "round gowns," which were gathered a short distance below the shoulders and thus did not require tight lacing. Like the great ladies, they were weighted down with jewelry; they wore long gold chains twined about their necks four or five times, their arms were adorned with bracelets and armlets, and their ears were hung with rings that sparkled with cheap gems.

The girls gathered in groups at street corners and joined the dandies in a kind of mass public flirting. Some of the youths carried bottles of port and little jugs of rum, and soon the girls were offering themselves at bargain prices, their customary shrewdness softened by the excitement and liquor.

In the general excitement over the coming of the redcoats there were pockets of calm. One of these was in the parlor of O'Neil's Tavern, where a little knot of respectable male citizens were gathered to discuss the business affairs of the city and to inveigh against the money changers of that modern Gomorrah known as New York.

There was a flurry in O'Neil's when the news came and was confirmed by a messenger dispatched to the War Department by a wealthy planter, but then the men returned to their generally approving discussion of the advances being made in public transportation.

The round table had been given impetus by a notice posted outside O'Neil's concerning the new service to be offered by the *Philadelphia, Baltimore and Washington City Lines.* This enterprising stage would undertake to carry a passenger from Washington to New York in three days for a fare of twenty-four dollars, not including meals and lodging. It was the consensus that this was a bargain, although there was some mur-

muring about the high price of a square meal en route, what with breakfast costing twenty-five cents, dinner sixty cents and supper thirty-five cents. And the beds were no better than they should have been, at seventy-five cents per night.

Nevertheless, there was a kind of small-boy wonderment, expressed in gruff tones, that a Washingtonian now could travel by stage to Boston in a week, and all the way to New Orleans in two days less than a month. Several of the group suggested, too, that the New Yorkers had hit upon a grand idea in their horse-boat, which ran every fifteen minutes between New York and Brooklyn and was able to make a profit at only four cents a passenger.

A real estate speculator named Van Ness said that something like that between Washington and Alexandria would be a contribution to progress. "It's not at all dear to operate," he pointed out. "All that is required are two horses to walk the treadmill that turns the paddle wheel."

Van Ness's remarks brought the talk around to steamboats, and a good laugh was enjoyed at the expense of Dr. William Thornton, Superintendent of the Patent Office. The men recalled now that it was Thornton, an inventor of considerable imagination, who had made John Fitch's steamboat run successfully on the Delaware in 1787—and yet the public interest had been so feeble that Thornton had neglected to take out patents. Then, in 1809, Robert Fulton had put very much the same boat on the Hudson and the public had gone wild with enthusiasm. Now steamboats plied the Hudson, Delaware and Potomac, and companies were forming to put them on the Mississippi and Ohio.

Plagued by the expense of doing business with businessmen

33

42732

in other cities, several of the group suggested that the steamboats eventually would reduce the cost of postage. The Post Office Department came under severe censure for the high postage rates as the suddenly irascible company mulled over this state of affairs: eight cents to send a single-sheet letter not more than thirty miles; ten cents for over thirty and not more than eighty miles; twelve and a half cents for over eighty and not more than a hundred and fifty miles, and eighteen and a half cents for letters going over one hundred and fifty but not more than four hundred miles. And, of course, an identical extra charge was made for each additional sheet mailed.

Someone suggested that "Madison should do something" about this appalling situation, and there was a roar of laughter. "Jemmy will be too busy for a while," one portly gentleman suggested. "He'll be running too fast to burden himself with any mail."

At the "President's House" or "President's Castle," President James Madison took time out from unhappy consultation with Secretary of War John Armstrong to gaze out the window and up Sixteenth Street, The cows grazing on the grounds of St. John's Church were the only inhabitants to remain unperturbed, and they seemed to set a wise example to the worried Madison.

"Perhaps the people should emulate those beasts," he told the burly Armstrong. "I greatly fear a panic."

Madison stood there, a man with solemn and unhandsome countenance, whose eyes wore their accustomed look of sadness. He was called the "Father of the Constitution," and he had served with distinction in Congress, where his writings and speeches were of unusual brilliance. Yet he realized his people

34

GERALD LIBRARY
COLBY JUNIOR COLLEGE
NEW LONDON, NEW HAMPSHIRE

had their doubts about his strength. After all, he was not an imposing figure; his small, wizened body stood only five feet six inches tall and his voice was soft and weak.

Armstrong looked down on the Virginian and commented, "I'll not get excited if that fool Winder will only keep his head."

Madison had not seen or heard from the capital's defender, Brigadier General William Henry Winder, commander of the Chesapeake Department of the United States Army.

"Where is Winder?" he asked Armstrong. "I presume he is busy, but he has not contacted me."

"Running about the city like a fool," replied Armstrong bitterly. He had not been consulted on Winder's appointment and he had washed his hands of any strategy Winder might evolve.

Armstrong was in a funk. He had argued with Madison that the British would never come to Washington, but now he was not so sure. He could only suggest tentatively that if the invaders appeared at the District line American troops should dig in at the Capitol and defend it as the British had defended the Chew Mansion in Germantown during the Revolutionary War.

Armstrong departed after a while, pleading "administrative detail." Madison sat there, consoled by the thought that at least one member of his Cabinet had shown an awareness of the peril in which the capital had been placed. Secretary of State James Monroe had visited him earlier and promised to do what he could to find somebody capable of taking the field and gathering intelligence about the movements of the invading force.

A feeling of acute indigestion intruded upon his thoughts.

The President's stomach was complaining about the heavy dinner he had eaten the night before. Dolly Madison had filled the dining room with government officials, prominent townspeople and diplomats, and had served a meal calculated to separate the men from the boys.

Madison groaned audibly now as he recalled the heavy and assorted victuals heaped in succession on that board. Fried eggs, fried beef, roast turkey, roast ducks, whole rounds of roast beef, that new foreign dish macaroni, several kinds of ices, mounds of cakes and tarts. The wines had been fine, but Madison had shown unwonted indiscretion in sampling the brandy.

It had been, in a sense, the fault of the French ambassador, the elegant M. Serurier. He had pressed a brandy on the President while relaying the latest rumors about British spies who reportedly had the run of the capital. His Majesty's representative had been especially intrigued by the report that a British agent had visited Dolly Madison disguised as a woman.

Perturbed, Madison had sent a liveried servant to ask Dolly to step their way for a moment. Shortly, Dolly glided into view, her handsome oval face glowing in the light of one thousand candles. Madison had noted that his wife looked particularly fetching in her yellow satin gown, which was embroidered all over with flights of butterflies. Nothing, he felt, set off her generous curves as satin did; but he had wanted her to take off that tall yellow turban so he could see her beautiful black hair.

Dolly had found the report ludicrous. "Nonsense," she'd said, gesturing with her snuff box. "I know personally every female who has been in this house for the past six months. I shall not suggest which would pass as males, since that is not the point."

M. Serurier bowed. Still, had not one heard of the spy who was "covered with leprosy, which was probably why he had turned traitor?" And his staff at Octagon House, which served France as a resplendent embassy, also had heard rumors of another agent who had conversed with Postmaster General Meigs in the latter's boardinghouse.

These days it seemed as if everybody who passed a moment with the President had a new spy story to tell. Mrs. William Thornton, wife of the Patent Office superintendent, had heard a batch of them at the Dancing Assembly the other evening and had relayed them to Madison at her first opportunity. The fact that they had circulated at the Dancing Assembly presumably gave the rumors respectability; after all, the Assembly had been organized as early as 1802 and therefore had tradition behind it.

Male guests at the President's House had passed along another passel of spy scares picked up in a more flamboyant quarter—at the suite maintained at O'Neill's Tavern by the notorious Major Robert Bailey. The florid major had come to Washington from Virginia's Berkeley Springs, where he had operated a popular gambling house, and over the tables in his hotel suite the plungers exchanged the latest reports of Britain's intelligence network.

Madison, whose only vice was horse racing, mildly disapproved of the patronage given Major Bailey by some of his high administration officials. He tried to understand their tastes, but it was difficult for a man who considered card games frivolous to regard gambling as a suitable pastime.

37

At times the nation over which he presided almost over-whelmed this gentle intellectual. Only thirty-eight years after the Declaration of Independence, these new United States suddenly had become an empire of continentlike proportions. With the purchase of the Louisiana Territory by Thomas Jefferson, the nation now boasted a total area of well over two million square miles, extending fifteen hundred miles from north to south and two thousand miles from east to west. Some of the more boastful citizenry called it the largest country in the civilized world save Imperial Russia.

Madison himself could not suppress a feeling of pride in this bustling, energetic country of eight million people. Eight million, that is, including more than a million slaves, he quickly reminded himself. The reminder directed his thoughts to the slave problem. He had never felt particularly uncomfortable about owning slaves himself, largely because the black folk at Montpelier and in his tobacco fields were treated with an unusual humaneness carefully observed by their master. And, of course, practically everybody of consequence was a slave-owner, too—Henry Clay, James Monroe, George Washington Campbell, the new Secretary of the Treasury, and Chief Justice John Marshall.

Now Madison told himself again that it was a problem that eventually would have to be settled, probably by nation-wide emancipation. Without quite explaining it to himself fully, he realized that slave labor would soon be without justification in a country which was making such rapid technical advances, a country whose stages made the run from Washington to Richmond in twenty-four hours, and where a steam railroad between New York and Philadelphia was already in the surveying stage.

However, the little President also saw that such a country might be a dangerous temptation to those who would wield tremendous power, and he was glad now that Pennsylvania's Senator William Maclay and other new Republicans had shouted down early efforts to give the President the title of "His Highness."

Unlike so many other Republicans, Madison had not accused the then Vice President, John Adams, of being a royalist for espousing the propriety of such titles as "His Highness" and "His Mightiness." He realized that the crusty Adams merely wanted to give the office the dignity and maturity that such a title would bestow. But Madison had voted for the simple "President of the United States" because he didn't want to give any Chief Executive an excuse for petty tyrannies.

It offended Madison that so many of the people still clung to the traditions of royalty. He cringed now at the thought that most of the ladies who visited the President's House persisted in referring to his cheerful Dolly as "Her Majesty" and the executive mansion as "The Palace," or "The Castle."

He *was* moody today, he told himself. Waiting for reports from Armstrong and Winder, he was assailed again by his hatred of war and by the incongruity which found him leading a nation in arms. He realized that his lack of enthusiasm prevented him from inspiring his nation as it should have been inspired in time of war. He knew the time demanded a lusty warrior who would act swiftly and inquire afterward as to the legality of his acts. But he could only watch the law and see that his powers were kept within the prescribed bounds.

Now, as the Ross-Cockburn expedition was poised to move against the capital, the old distrust of Armstrong and Winder returned. He wondered if the militia assigned to defend Washington would fight willingly under these men—one brooding and quarrelsome, the other uncertain and too concerned with being a hail-fellow to work with the unceasing conscientiousness his heavy chore demanded.

[III]

Defenders of the Capital

THIS CURIOUS WAR had contrived to place the defense of Washington in the hands of two curious military leaders—Secretary of War Armstrong and Brigadier General Winder—who were neither really qualified nor mutually compatible.

John Armstrong's appointment to the War Portfolio in February 1813 had amazed Washington. He was a man with a proven reputation for unreliability and undercover plotting, and his hostility to Madison had become well known. History subsequently would decide that he got the post because he was an officer in the Revolution and because, as a New Yorker, he helped balance a Cabinet dominated by Virginians like Secretary of State James Monroe.

Northerners had been particularly outraged that Monroe had doubled as War Secretary for six weeks early in 1813 before Armstrong took over. And the erudite Federalist Josiah Quincy of Massachusetts had complained in the House that the government was conducted by "two Virginians and a foreigner," the latter being the Swiss Secretary of the Treasury, Albert Gallatin.

Armstrong had abandoned his studies at Princeton at the start of the Revolutionary War and soon became an aide to General Hugh Mercer, an old friend of George Washington. Mercer was mortally wounded on the Princeton battlefield in January 1777, and it was Armstrong who carried the dying general from the battlefield to a nearby farmhouse and remained with him until death came.

Fate was unkind to the eighteen-year-old Armstrong in his next assignment, for he became aide-de-camp to General Horatio Gates, a long-time schemer against Washington. It was Gates who prevailed upon the young American to write the infamous—and anonymous—"Newburgh Letters" in 1783 when the Army was at Newburgh, New York. The letters called for a mutiny against Washington and the use of force in "persuading" Congress to hand over to the troops their back pay.

It was not until some time after the war ended that Armstrong admitted authorship of the letters. But Washington, then President, was most lenient with the young man; he offered the suggestion that Armstrong had been under bad influences and was not aware of the harm his letters could have caused the nation.

While serving with Gates, Armstrong had given further evidence of his poor judgment by becoming close friends with Gates's adjutant general, James Wilkinson. Wilkinson was deeply involved in the conspiracy against Washington, and after the Revolutionary War he committed himself to a career of chicanery and treasonable activities. His name was on a secret Spanish payroll while he was commanding a department of the United States Army, and he was proved to have accepted several mule-loads of doubloons. He joined Aaron Burr in his intrigue, then turned state's evidence.

When the War of 1812 began, Wilkinson was back in New Orleans, drinking heavily, a frequenter of the lower-class gambling hells, a neurotic hypochondriac whose spells of imaginary sickness confined him to his bed for days at a time. Yet, in the summer of 1813, Armstrong had appointed him commander of the northern army to replace the unfortunate Major General Henry (Granny) Dearborn.

"Why should you remain in your land of cypress when patriotism and ambition equally invite to one where grows the laurel," Armstrong wrote Wilkinson. "Again the men of the North and East want you. I speak to you with a frankness due to you and to myself, and again advise, come to the North, and come quickly! If our cards be well played we may renew the scene of Saratoga."

The eminence which was Armstrong's as the British expedition prepared to march on the capital had been achieved circuitously. After the Revolution, he studied law, served as Attorney General of Pennsylvania and sat in the House for that commonwealth in the first Federal Congress in 1787. He made a politically fortunate marriage in 1789 to Alida Livingston, sister of Robert R. Livingston, entrepreneur, politician and sometime minister to France. There followed eleven years of farming in Duchess County, New York.

Armstrong called himself a Federalist, but his loyalties always were skin deep. When he returned to public affairs it was as the author of a vitriolic letter demanding the repeal of the Alien and Sedition Laws passed by his Federalist friends. Armstrong now decided he was a Republican and allied himself with George Clinton.

This alliance permitted him to serve in the United States Senate from New York, and his connection with the Livingston family led to his succeeding Robert Livingston as American minister to Paris in 1804. In that post he was a gullible flop, a bumbling farmer who got lost in the mazes of diplomacy. Napoleon called him "ridiculous," and complained that he "wrote things that no one can comprehend."

Returning to America, Armstrong had another surprise to spring—this time on his friend, De Witt Clinton. He took the stump against Clinton and supported the re-election of President Madison in 1812. In return, Madison appointed him a brigadier general commanding the militia charged with the defense of New York City. Whereupon Armstrong turned on Madison by discouraging enlistments in the Regular Army in order to build up his own militia. In his spare time, which seemed limitless, Armstrong became an active and outspoken opponent of the Virginian "dynasty" headed by Madison, whose heir apparent was James Monroe. The result was that, when Armstrong joined the Cabinet, he spent most of his time intriguing against Monroe while the American war effort wilted from lack of leadership.

Yet at the time of Armstrong's appointment, Madison felt he had no other choice. He believed that Armstrong possessed "a degree of military information which might be useful," and he told friends he hoped this would compensate for Armstrong's "objectionable peculiarities." Besides, Armstrong was a Northerner.

It was as a Northerner, of course, that sections of the country south of Philadelphia suspected Armstrong. Maryland was bitter about his inability or unwillingness to stop Cockburn's depredations in the Chesapeake. One Baltimore newspaper was incredulous. "Will the people of the United States believe," it asked, "that a strong, regular force has been, for the past three weeks, within fifty miles of an enemy laying waste the whole country and that the Secretary of War has not, although repeatedly solicited, ordered a solitary individual to our assistance?"

Many people believed that Armstrong's repeated criticisms of Washington as a location for the capital indicated he would make no attempt to defend the city. The New York *Post* said of Washington residents, "They think the Secretary of War wishes to have the seat of government removed, that he may destroy the Virginia combination, which now stands in the way of his promotion to the next Presidency."

Later, the *Post* reported: "We understand that General Armstrong has given it as his opinion that the city of Washington cannot be defended; and it is said he has engaged quarters in Carlisle [Pennsylvania], to which place it is supposed he will retreat should the British make their appearance in the District."

And, "Armstrong is suspected and cursed by almost every

person here in Washington. Deputations have . . . declared to the President their total want of confidence in Armstrong . . . Armstrong and some others in power will be well watched. If any disaster befall the District . . . they may not from the present temper of the people find it easy to escape."

Meanwhile, Armstrong's appointment already had caused Madison to lose one of his most competent Cabinet members. Secretary of the Treasury Gallatin, regarded by many as the young nation's most brilliant public servant, looked on Armstrong as corrupt and mentally retarded. He was already disgusted with Congress's demands that he raise money for the war without damaging anybody's pocketbook, and the Armstrong appointment was the last straw.

Gallatin went to Madison and resigned on the same day Armstrong's appointment was announced. Madison pleaded with him to stay, but Gallatin was icily adamant. To give the parting a cloak of harmony, however, Gallatin suggested he be named to the American peace delegation which was about to sail for Europe to participate in a movement of international conciliation. Madison reluctantly made the appointment and Gallatin had sailed in May 1813 for Russia.

Monroe, who maintained a rigid belief that ability and merit should come before all political considerations, was outraged by Armstrong's appointment and the subsequent loss of Gallatin. Madison, by sheer necessity, was a shrewder politician who sadly acknowledged that a President had sometimes to sacrifice competence in order to lessen the strain on a still fragile union of jealous and independent states.

Quietly he pointed out to Monroe that although Virginia still was the most populous state, with 974,000 people, New York had climbed into second place with 959,000. And the largest cities were in Armstrong's North—New York with 96,000 and Philadelphia with 92,000. With those statistics in mind, it behooved a President with an unpopular war on his hands to seek support wherever he could find it.

The nation's share of misfortune was further increased by having Brigadier General William Henry Winder in command of the defense of Washington. General Winder was a tall man of brawny handsomeness and amiable disposition who was better suited for politics than for the military. A Marylander, he studied at the University of Pennsylvania and then read for the law in the office of his uncle, John Henry, who had served in the Continental Congress during the Revolution. After passing the bar, Winder spent a brief sojourn in Tennessee but felt uncomfortable among the frontiersmen and returned to Maryland. There he was elected, at the age of twenty-three, to the Maryland legislature from his home county of Somerset. Later, he established a law practice in Baltimore, where his pleasing manner and fluent speech enabled him to talk himself into a brigadier general's commission. This was most unfortunate for the country, for Winder shortly proved that his military abilities were overshadowed by an extreme caution that bordered on timidity.

Winder muffed his chance for glory on a day in June 1813. He was commanding a brigade in the Northern Theater at a time when General Dearborn had established a foothold on the Canadian border. There was hope then, with England's General John Vincent in hasty retreat, that the whole of Upper Canada would fall to the United States. Dearborn sent General

47

Winder with 800 troops in pursuit of Vincent, who had pulled up at his supply base at Burlington Heights.

Winder, moving with a kind of apologetic reluctance, marched half the forty miles to Burlington Heights, then sat down and started to worry. He became convinced his force was not large enough for the chore at hand and demanded reinforcements. Dearborn sent Brigadier General John Chandler with another 500 men. Temporarily fortified, Winder advanced another ten miles and came to another halt at Stony Creek. Here he set up a disorderly camp, with a haphazard picket that could offer no genuine protection.

Vincent, ten miles ahead, was intrigued by Winder's slow advance and he decided on a flurry to see what manner of men were pursuing him. Vincent had only 600 men, less than half the combined Winder-Chandler force, but he struck with a surprise attack early in the morning of June 6, and the assault demoralized the Americans. Most of them fled back toward Fort George, but Generals Winder and Chandler remained guests of the British, victims of two of the most humiliating captures in American military history.

Chandler was hurt by a fall from his horse and wandered into a British party. Winder, apparently unaware of how the fight was going, saw some men standing by a cannon and walked over to talk to them. Too late he perceived that they were wearing red coats and were, in fact, the same detachment which earlier had captured Chandler.

But Winder was the kind of man who could fall into a mud hole and come up clutching a handful of emeralds. At the Beauport jail near Quebec, his amiability soon won him friends among the more high-ranking of his captors who were trying to arrange a *modus operandi* for an exchange of prisoners. By invitation, Winder took part in these discussions and his legal talents came up with some ideas which the British found sound. Governor General Sir George Prevost, the Crown's agent, gave Winder a sixty-day parole and sent him off to Washington with the proposals.

In the capital, Winder conferred at length with Madison, who was too preoccupied with the matter at hand to mention the general's disgrace at Stony Point. Besides, Madison had been impressed by the newspapers' account of the ovation Winder had received in his adopted city of Baltimore when he stopped there en route. Winder's proposals seemed the only practicable solution to the exchange problem and Winder was sent back to Quebec to continue his consultations with Prevost.

When Madison finally accepted the exchange plan, Winder was released and started back to Washington to report for duty. Just past Baltimore he was accosted by a most unexpected hitchhiker, General James Wilkinson. Wilkinson also was bound for Washington, to testify at a court-martial he had requested in order to determine whether he or John Armstrong had been responsible for the collapse of the recent campaign against Canada.

Wilkinson had started from Baltimore on horseback but had become ill shortly after leaving the city. Unable to go farther on his jouncing steed, he had taken a stand on the road to beg a ride the rest of the way. Winder made room in his carriage and the two rode into Washington together.

Picking up Wilkinson almost proved disastrous for Winder. When he arrived in the capital Madison was about to appoint a commander of the Chesapeake Department and Winder's name was high on the list. It was late June 1814, and the President was determined to reorganize the city's defenses. But Madison heard of Winder's companionship with Wilkinson and was taken aback. Hastily he sent an agent to determine whether the veteran of the Stony Creek fiasco was on close terms with the unsavory Wilkinson. Apparently Winder and his friends convinced the emissary that he had merely performed an act of mercy in rescuing the stranded Wilkinson.

Yet even though he was cleared of this disparaging connection, it is probably true that Winder was appointed partly because he happened to arrive at Washington when the other eligibles were serving on distant grounds. Fortune was playing a sad joke on the President by converting Winder's military failure into an opportunity for an even more ill-advised assignment.

There were also several political aspects which influenced Madison's decision. Winder was a cousin to Governor Levin Winder of Maryland, a Federalist and one of the leading critics of the military's inability to drive Admiral Cockburn from the Chesapeake. Madison believed that the appointment of General Winder would appease the governor, and that the noisy reception the general had received in Baltimore would win him the support of Maryland in any defensive moves he made for the protection of the general neighborhood.

Admittedly, Madison was taking a risk, and he had to agree with the conclusions of former President Jefferson, who had written him from Monticello a wry comment on the difficulty of finding competent military leadership: "The Creator has not thought proper to mark those on the forehead who are of the stuff to make good generals. We are first, therefore, to seek them, blindfolded, and then let them learn the trade at the expense of great losses." Now Madison hoped that his country would not have to pay too high a price.

[IV]

Rally to the Cause

MADISON HAD ANTICIPATED some of these problems two
months before when he had voiced his apprehension over the
fall of Napoleon and his exile to Elba.

It had been at a typically brilliant Dolly Madison dinner
at the White House on a balmy night in June 1814. Everybody
who counted was there—and a few of the poorer Republicans
who were uncounted by the mighty but who happened to be
good friends of Jemmy Madison.

The talk was all of the Corsican's defeat and the Allies' triumphal entry into Paris. Curiously, those Americans present were gleeful over Napoleon's fall, despite the fact that he had been a strong—albeit selfish—ally against Great Britain in America's second war with her mother country.

Even Madison, antimonarchist that he was, seemed relieved at the defeat of the squat dictator. He had always been uncomfortable taking sides with a tyrant as evil to him as the kings he despised. Yet he had his misgivings, and they were serious ones, affecting the well-being of his own nation. For the defeat of Napoleon meant that a large number of Wellington's troops was made available for service against the United States.

In a quiet corner, after the brandy, Madison voiced his fears to his youthful Attorney General, Richard Rush, and his Secretary of War, John Armstrong. Madison suggested that defense plans be drawn up against new landings of British troops; he even offered the tentative thought that perhaps the capital itself might be in danger.

Rush was thoughtful but noncommittal; he said only that the matter should be considered carefully. But Armstrong, outwardly bluff and plain-spoken, inwardly devious and smallminded, a plotter against Madison, scoffed at the President's fears.

"Washington in danger!" he said. "It's preposterous. The British will never come here. If they try at any city it will be Baltimore—a much more important port."

Madison remained concerned, but he did not press his point; Armstrong was a hard man to talk to. Unhappily, the President had no way of knowing that only a few days earlier a squadron

of eleven ships-of-war had dropped down the Garonne River
from Bordeaux, bound for Bermuda and, eventually, the Chesapeake. The ships carried 2,800 veterans of the Peninsula campaign, plucked from Wellington's forces to form the nucleus
of an expedition for the chastisement of America.

A man of great mental precision, whose thoughts often
troubled him as he pondered the incongruities of life, Madison
continued to brood on the weird circumstances which could
cause a nation to celebrate the downfall of an ally. But then,
he told himself, this was a weird, a most incongruous war in
which the United States found itself.

Historians, Madison mused, would be justified in calling it
the strangest war in history. Although New England shipping
had been all but ruined by the British impressment of American
seamen and blockade of the shipping lanes, the warmongers
had come from the South and new West.

Madison smiled at the thought of the then Speaker of the
House, Henry Clay, representative of buckskin-clad Ken-
tuckians, standing up in the House as a vociferous champion of
free trade and sailors' rights. It was canny of Clay, of course;
he had realized the necessity for putting his war with England
in a package that would be attractive to the populous North-
eastern and Central Atlantic states.

And Madison acknowledged the validity of Clay's real concern—the threat to the new West and South of the British conspiracy with the stalwart Indian chief Tecumseh. It had been
Tecumseh's dream to establish an independent Indian state from
the Great Lakes to the Gulf of Mexico and the British Cabinet
had eagerly fallen in with the scheme.

Clay's War Hawks had been accused of seeking war with

England as an excuse to annex Canada and obtain more territory and trade, but Madison had never run with that pack. He was aware that British traders and factors had fomented Indian uprisings and he knew Clay feared a British protectorate over the projected Indian state. The President was convinced that Clay's war aim was security, not greed.

Moreover, Madison recognized that Clay, a genuine nationalist, felt an honest concern for the impressed seamen. The President had always been impressed by the Kentuckian's vision of America's glorious destiny. He could not rebuke a man of such sincerity merely because he had found it expedient to use sailors' rights as a means of bringing on the war that to him meant the securing of safety for the frontier folk.

Madison reminded himself now that, after all, he had not opposed the final resort to war. He had tried to prevent it, to the point of being accused of timidity and charged with treason, but he had been determined to call the nation to arms if no other recourse presented itself. Clay's colorful rhetoric, his ability to dramatize the issue, had won the votes necessary to declare war, but Madison was content in the knowledge that he had yielded slowly and had finally given way only when he had become convinced that further negotiations were useless.

He knew the city was filled with pro-British propagandizers who had fanned up hatred for "Jemmy Madison's War," although Madison felt that the notoriety rightfully belonged to Clay, and that the people should be calling it "Henry Clay's War" instead. Anonymous threats and warnings had been received by Dolly herself, informing her that if she and her husband attempted to quit the President's House in case of attack they would be stopped and shot. He wished that Monroe were around to strengthen his self-confidence.

Secretary of State Monroe was too busy at the moment—although not with the duties officially prescribed for him by his title. He was devoted to the art of diplomacy and to his own efforts to plant respect for his country in the world's capitals. But his boundless energy found the routine of the State Department stultifying; he often commented that the five clerks assigned to him were four too many.

Moreover, Monroe's service in the Revolutionary War had launched him on a lifetime romance with the military. He had been critically wounded at Trenton but this failed to dampen his enthusiasm, and he was discharged as a lieutenant colonel; his friends called him Colonel, not Mister Secretary.

Now with Washington threatened, Monroe yearned to take to the field once more, to leave the intricacies of diplomacy for the clean-cut issues and swift decisions of the battlefield. Besides, like Madison, he distrusted both Armstrong and Winder as do-nothings. What the American forces needed immediately was information about what the enemy was doing, and Monroe had no faith in the American leaders' ability to obtain it.

Monroe took to the saddle and rode up Pennsylvania Avenue to Capitol Hill to think. There, he let his horse jog him about the grounds while he pondered the problem of persuading somebody to act. Soon he dismounted and entered the Capitol building, making his way to the gloomy basement chamber beneath the Senate floor where the Supreme Court met in season. He wanted a couple of ounces of rum and he knew a court clerk who kept it handy.

Lounging on one of the new Sheraton chairs, he sipped his

rum and chatted with the law clerk. The clerk had a new story about the justices and it refreshed Monroe's mind to hear it. Like most court stories of the time, it concerned the justices' appreciation of an occasional spirituous nip during working hours.

There had been criticism of this by the more Puritanical in the government family, and Chief Justice John Marshall had compromised with public opinion; he decreed there would be no drinking on Saturdays, except in case of rain.

The following Saturday, the justices had hardly begun their work when the Chief Justice cleared his throat and asked Justice Storey to "please look out the window and decide whether there be any sign of rain."

Justice Storey solemnly walked to the window and then came back sadly shaking his head. "There is no sign of rain," he announced.

The Chief Justice seemed appalled. "Justice Storey," he said, "I have never heard a more shallow or illogical opinion. You forget that the United States is a vast country—a very vast country—and that our jurisdiction is just as broad as the country itself. By the laws of nature, it must be raining somewhere in our jurisdiction and this court takes judicial notice of the laws of nature. This court finds, therefore, that it is raining, and orders the waiter to bring on the rum."

Monroe laughed appreciatively, put down his empty glass, and got up to go. He had made up his mind to take matters into his own hands.

A Virginian, Monroe wasted no thoughts on the Washington or Maryland militia. He wanted men of spirit and daring and to him that meant his fellow Virginians. Happily, he spurred his

horse and galloped off to Alexandria where he pulled to a jarring stop before the headquarters of one Captain Thornton's
Alexandria militia troop. The good captain made the rounds
with him and they spent the night of the eighteenth of August
mustering twenty-five men of the troop to take to their saddles
in search of the enemy.

Next morning at dawn, Monroe and his scouting force galloped off on their reconnaissance. They rode through pine
forests and through pasturelands, across green meadows and
splashingly through creeks made low by the summer's heat.
Here and in the low surrounding hills, they spread out to search
thoroughly the Potomac and Patuxent neighborhoods.

The first day their only piece of intelligence turned out to be
incorrect. A farm family traveling in a hay wagon passed the
startling word that the enemy already had reached Lower
Marlborough. Monroe distrusted this information and dispatched a five-man patrol to check. The patrol joined the main
body that evening with word that Lower Marlborough still was
thoroughly American, though fearful.

Monroe, unaware that General Ross's invading force had no
cavalry, posted a strong picket line that night against any surprise attack by an advance enemy guard. He remained awake
most of the night himself, mentally reviewing the day's patrol
to make sure his combing action had not by-passed any avenue
by which the invaders could approach the capital. At dawn the
next morning—August 20—the patrol was on its way again.

At ten o'clock, Monroe's patrol found the enemy—still at
Benedict. The Secretary of State turned his force back to a hiding place a safe distance away, then himself took up a post in a
pine forest overlooking the debarkation point. With a telescope,

he watched the troops in their scarlet jackets leaving their ships, and inspected their camp on the grassy slopes above the town.

His eyes found one of the three cannon with which Ross would take up his march, but he had no way of knowing it represented one third of the Britons' artillery. Vainly, he searched the area for signs of horses. He couldn't believe it possible that the troops were entirely on foot but there it was; there was no sign even of a pack mule.

Monroe sent reports to Madison that day and that night by special couriers. Included in one of the pouches was a letter written by one of the Alexandria officers, a sometime journalist, who requested that Madison forward it to the New York *Post* after scanning its contents.

"I am now with Mr. Monroe," the letter said. "We have this morning reconnoitered the enemy in every direction, and collected every information which the neighborhood affords. At ten o'clock A.M. this day we had full view of all their shipping which lay from Benedict to about eight miles below. I counted 23 ships, several brigs and some few small craft.

"The barges and a number of schooners and three large vessels (say frigates) had proceeded up the river toward Nottingham before we got our stand. From the best information I can get I believe the whole force landed at Benedict is about 6,000. The distress of the neighborhood is inconceivable."

Monroe's messages to Madison also estimated the enemy force at 6,000, a surprisingly close approximation of the actual number of just over 5,000.

The sight of the enemy disembarking and of their tidy camp was impressive, but Monroe felt a new confidence surging in him. He knew the American command could muster at least

59

7,000 men with adequate artillery, and he felt sure this force could repulse any attempt to take the capital, particularly since Ross would have to sacrifice a detachment en route to protect his supply line and his line of retreat. Monroe sent some of his men back to Washington, but remained in the pine forest with the rest of the troop to await further developments.

Monroe's confidence that Washington could be successfully defended would seem to have been justified. Against a British force which would be reduced by the exigencies of prudent warfare to less than 4,000 men by the time it reached the capital, General Winder could count on mustering almost 7,000. To be sure, only a thousand or so would be regular troops, and the militia was rusty from idleness, but the numerical advantage of the Americans still seemed impressive.

Moreover, the Americans had a tremendous advantage in artillery, with 26 guns available within the different militia companies, compared to the three cannon and the rocket tubes General Ross carried with him. Even Madison, much less ebullient than his Secretary of State, was comforted by these figures, while brooding about the quality of the troops' leadership and their questionable reputation as first-class fighting men.

General Winder impressed the citizenry with his intense activity. He dashed from meeting to meeting, rode about the city conferring with assorted military commanders and on his infrequent stops at his desk scribbled a long series of general orders.

Specifically, he called out the District of Columbia militia, summoning it to mobilize on Friday night, August 19, at the Tiber River, an inconsequential stream just west of Capitol

Hill. The militia consisted of two brigades and was commanded by John P. Van Ness, a militia major general and a prominent banker and property owner.

During the past year, Van Ness had nagged War Secretary Armstrong ceaselessly, demanding improvement in the city's defenses, but Armstrong had maintained that the British would never come to Washington. Now he called on Armstrong again, confident that with the British about to march, the Secretary of War finally would be convinced of Washington's danger.

Armstrong was sitting at his desk, the sweat dripping from his red face. But he was still the same old Armstrong.

"Oh, yes, by God!" roared the Secretary. "They would not come with such a fleet without meaning to strike somewhere, but they certainly will not come here. What in the devil will they do here?"

Van Ness restrained a violent impulse. He explained as calmly as he could that the capture of the United States capital would be a worthy accomplishment for an army seeking to demoralize its enemy.

"No, no!" shouted Armstrong. "I tell you, Baltimore is the place, sir. That city is of much more consequence. Try to remember your military strategy, sir."

Van Ness was furious. Already doubtful about Winder's abilities, he now was convinced that Armstrong was an idiotic poltroon who could not be counted on to take command. He went to Madison with the demand that the President relieve Winder and assign Washington's defense to him, Van Ness.

Madison explained that this was no time to switch commands; there was too much to be done. Whereupon Van Ness resigned his commission. Madison named as his successor Brigadier

General Walter Smith of Georgetown, who would be subject to Winder's orders.

The President's next visitor was General Wilkinson, at liberty while he awaited his court-martial. Wilkinson asked that his arrest be temporarily lifted so he could offer his services.

The onetime plotter and secret Spanish agent talked military common sense. He pointed out that the country through which General Ross must march was well settled, with numerous crossroads which offered excellent opportunities for ambushes, and that it abounded in defiles, ravines and streams which could be turned into formidable obstacles in the path of the invading force.

"Why," Wilkinson told Madison, "one hundred men with axes could fell enough trees along Ross's route to delay him for days."

Madison thanked Wilkinson for his offer of assistance and for his ideas, which he told the general were excellent. But he regretfully had to refuse Wilkinson's services. Privately, he was afraid the general would further confuse a situation already threatening to become chaotic.

Wilkinson was crushed, but he continued to plead his plan of action. "Mr. President," he urged, "have Armstrong see to it that the roads in the enemy's front are blocked. Then he should send a force around Ross to fall on his rear, while flying detachments harass his flanks. We must fight like Indians."

Madison thanked Wilkinson again. Then, when the general had taken his leave, the President dictated a message to Armstrong, telling him of Wilkinson's plan and expressing the opinion that it was sound. Armstrong read and filed it.

General Winder apparently was too distracted by his worries

about the defensive inadequacies around the capital to think about trying to impede the British march. He kept sending couriers with urgent messages calling on the militia of Maryland, Virginia and Pennsylvania to rally to Washington's defense.

A force of thirteen regiments had been drafted in those three states as early as June, but the agreement was that they were not to be called into active service "until the enemy should appear." Winder had protested to Armstrong in vain against this arrangement; he had urged that the men be called at once and be assigned to take up positions between Washington and the Chesapeake and around Baltimore. There, he argued, they could be drilled and disciplined and thus be ready for action when danger threatened.

A little foresight several months before might have considerably eased the situation. In late June, a regular army force of 500 men recruited in North Carolina had encamped in Washington. They were topflight fighting material and were commanded by Colonel Duncan L. Clinch, a Regular Army officer who had served brilliantly against the British on the border and against the Seminoles. But while Armstrong presumably was looking for men to defend the capital, this force was sent to the Canadian border.

The District of Columbia Militia assembled on Friday night, the nineteenth, as ordered. General Smith was appalled at what he saw. Few of the men had uniforms. Worse, many of them were without weapons of any kind. A number of them were barefoot. Smith dismissed them peremptorily and told them to return the following morning.

"Find some shoes," he told them, "and if you can't lay your hands on a gun, steal a butcher knife somewhere."

"By God," Smith said to his quartermaster, "how does that blockhead Armstrong expect me to fight a battle with scarecrows like that!" The general wanted to know what equipment the quartermaster could supply from Federal stores.

"Federal stores?" repeated the quartermaster. "We've barely got enough to feed the men. I haven't seen any shoes at all and we've been expecting new muskets for two weeks. It's almost impossible to lay your hands on any wagons because they're all being used to transport people's furniture out of town."

Smith cursed heavily, then had the officers detain the men and read them a lecture on patriotic self-sacrifice. The general cited, possibly with tongue in cheek, an order in florid prose issued by General Winder: "Let no man allow his private opinions, his prejudices or caprices in favor of this or that particular arm or weapon to be excuses for deserting his post, but seize on those which can be furnished him, or he can command himself, in order to resolutely encounter the enemy, and prove that the bravery of free men fighting for their families, their liberties, can render every weapon formidable."

Next morning the troops showed up again, with slightly better equipment. One of them, Joseph McGuane of Georgetown, brandished two axes and a bullwhip.

However raffish their appearance and their equipment, the militia were heroes to the Washington newspapers. Wedging it in with advertisements offering a 38-ounce loaf of bread for 12 cents and the services of a chimney sweep at 44 cents "for a high house," the *National Intelligencer* paid its tribute to "those thousands of brave men" who it said were prepared to "resist the host of mercenaries that now threatens us.

"Great as the public anxiety must naturally be at such a time, all look with confidence to the capacity and vigilance of the Commanding General, and we feel no doubt that his foresight and activity will leave nothing undone that our security requires."

Winder's efforts were aided by Secretary of the Navy William Jones, who sent a courier to the swashbuckling Commodore Joshua Barney at Pig Point to destroy his little flotilla of gunboats should the British turn toward Washington. Jones reasoned that Barney and his five hundred hardened seamen would be much more use lined up with the defenders of the capital than in trying to defend his barges from Admiral Cockburn's gunboats and Marines.

Commodore Barney was one of the few authentic fighting men the Americans could boast in the Chesapeake area. He had begun his career on a pilot boat at the age of twelve and at twenty he performed a feat of naval warfare that won him the hearts of the nation and a kiss from Marie Antoinette.

Commanding the *Hyder-Ally*, with 110 men and 16 six-pounders, Barney captured the British sloop-of-war *General Monk* off the Cape of Delaware. For this he won a gold-hilted sword from the city of Philadelphia and was the hero of an overnight ballad:

> *Come all ye lads that know no fear,*
> *To wealth and honor we will steer,*
> *In the* Hyder-Ally *privateer,*
> *Commanded by bold Barney.*

When Barney sailed the *General Monk* to France to sell it for prize money, he was swept up by the ladies at Versailles. Marie Antoinette's hearty kiss was delivered in front of a large audience, resulting in a popular song, "Barney, Leave the Girls Alone."

Barney was aboard the *Andrea Doria* in 1776 when, at St. Eustatius in the West Indies, the Dutch governor delivered the first salute in history to the new American flag. And it was Barney, in France when the British representatives and Benjamin Franklin signed the documents recognizing American independence, who brought home the first news of that great event.

When the War of 1812 began, Barney went back to privateering with his schooner *Rossie*, captured fifteen British prizes and sank another nine. This brought him his commission of captain of the Chesapeake fleet, a curious squadron consisting of fourteen old scows and barges.

Admiral Cockburn sneered at Barney, but the commodore changed the expression on the admiral's face by keeping a sizable portion of Cockburn's fleet occupied with a series of swift, harassing strikes. In one of these actions, Barney's fleet chased the British schooner *St. Lawrence* and half a dozen smaller craft most of the way down Chesapeake Bay until the British craft found refuge under the seventy-four guns of the warship *Dragon*.

Now it appeared that Commodore Barney would do his fighting on land. If he got into action, the British would be well aware of it.

[V]

Redcoats on the March

FINALLY, AFTER TWO DAYS, the British were ready to march, and the bugles' blast came at an inopportune moment for Lieutenant George Robert Gleig of His Majesty's 85th Light Infantry Regiment.

Gleig had grown restless on the morning of August 20 and had gone on a foraging expedition. He and his companions had been able to buy a chicken from an old woman trying to repair her cottage after the havoc wreaked by looters, and when they got back to town about noon they found another officer had wangled a pig, a duck and another chicken. They were just sitting down to a good meal when the bugles sounded. Soldierlike, each took as much bread and meat in his hand as he could manage; they stowed the rest in haversacks and hurried off to their stations.

As the army grouped for the advance, Gleig was surprised to discover that it included a detachment of a hundred Negroes, all armed with muskets, some with fixed bayonets. General Ross had orders not on any account to directly encourage American slaves to rebel against their masters, lest unorganized bands of slaves indulge in a reign of terror for which England would be blamed. Instead, he was told to accept any Negroes who volunteered for service with the British forces and to use them for both labor duty and combat. Most of the Negroes had been picked up during Cockburn's excursions ashore and had been drilled by seamen aboard ship.

With the units in formation, General Ross now rode up to get the march under way. He was greeted by a roar of cheering which seemed at first to embarrass him. But he recovered, swept off his hat and bowed to his men.

Smilingly, Ross asked the troops if they were ready to advance. A thunder of "ayes" answered him.

"Then let us be on our way," Ross told them quietly. "We have much to do."

The impressionable Gleig admitted later that the scene had given him "a fair lump" in his throat.

For the march, General Ross had brigaded his army. Light troops were withdrawn from three regiments and, with the 85th, were formed into a Light Brigade commanded by Colonel

William Thornton, chief of the 85th. Thus Gleig found himself in the advance guard.

The companies marched in an order which reflected General Ross's fear of ambushes. That is, two companies marched along the road while a third formed an advance scouting party and provided men to cover the flanks—which in this case put them in the heavily wooded areas on both sides of the road.

Gleig took a look at the situation and decided the Americans would be insane if they didn't attempt an ambush. He noticed that all sorts of paths led through the woods over which small bodies of riflemen could move unconcealed until they were upon the British advance.

"Let us hope," he told an officer named Charlton, "that the Americans are short on enterprise these days. These woods were created for the kind of attacks favored by Indians."

Charlton was sure the Americans would harass them. "They're so boastful of their rifles and their marksmanship," he said. "Here is their opportunity to show off their skills."

However, the column marched the rest of the day without seeing a single American. It was as if they were marching through a wilderness, despite an occasional cottage by the side of the road. Gleig, an eager soldier, was nonetheless satisfied; the marchers were having enough trouble with the humid Maryland heat.

Despite the fact that most of the troops had served in Spain, they had never experienced anything like the torrid mugginess that now enwrapped them like a steaming cloak. There was not a breath of air, the sun seemed to be burning a hole in the sky, while the deep sand of the road filled the air with dust from the constant tread of the marching feet. Those making their

69

way through the woods were torn by briars, and the high grass seemed to enclose the heat around them.

To make things worse, of course, men and officers both were loaded down with three days' provisions, eighty rounds of ball cartridges, haversacks and other equipment. After three months of idleness and freedom from forced marches, the men also had grown a trifle soft, and some of the best of the troops were dropping by the wayside, unable to continue. Discipline was relaxed enough to let the men stop and drink from the streams they passed, but still it was an exhausted army that paused for the night shortly after sunset.

Gleig was assigned to one of the outposts about a quarter of a mile in advance of the camp. He found this to be a farmhouse with assorted barns and outbuildings, commanded like a military post by an old man with a rough tongue. He was the only human being on the place, and not a very agreeable one. Clearly, he was a thoroughgoing Yankee and a good democrat. He denounced the invasion in cuss words Gleig had never heard before, and assured the British post "you'll get the stuffings knocked out of you."

Gleig rather enjoyed the aged Yankee's attitude. Until then, the few Americans he had encountered had acted like scared rabbits and he was glad to find someone who wasn't afraid to stick up for his own country.

"After all, most of these people are Englishmen," Gleig told Charlton. "I don't like to see them acting in such a cowardly fashion. Except for this old man, the Americans don't seem to be the same people who won their revolution."

Although the old man continued to berate his British guests, Gleig felt a sudden affection for him. He found himself hoping that if the positions were reversed he would be just as belligerent as this aged Yankee. And, apparently, the old man was also enjoying himself. He produced a crock of what he called "peach whiskey" and some bread and cheese, and invited the Englishmen to join him in a meal. While they ate, the old man pursued his denunciation of everything British and boasted that his two sons had left home that very morning to join the army and help administer a whipping to the redcoats.

Gleig was too conscientious an officer to let his pickets stay the night indoors and he spent most of the night with them in the clearing adjoining the barnyard. That night, the entire British Army was drenched by a two-hour thunderstorm, about which Gleig later wrote: "The effect of such a storm, echoed back as it was from the thick woods around, was awful in no ordinary degree; whilst every flash of lightning gave to the eye a momentary glimpse of scenery such as no powers of language are adequate to describe."

General Ross's pickets understandably could not be expected to share Gleig's appreciation of a countryside illuminated in such a turbulent fashion. Most of the men, in fact, were too busy grumbling over what they believed was a superfluous show of caution by their commander.

Indeed, Ross was taking no chances. Although most commanders would have assigned a relatively few pickets at strategic points, Ross in effect had girdled the entire encampment with them. The pickets were stationed about one hundred yards from the picket station to which they belonged, and stood about fifty yards apart in a great manmade circle.

Except on the road, the pickets stood alone; on the road they were stationed in pairs so that one soldier could make a periodic patrol ahead of the army to check on possible Yankee activity. All picket officers were required to check their sentinels regularly to make certain they kept awake.

Gleig was faithful to his trust, making his rounds doggedly even at the height of the storm, a performance of duty which seemed superfluous to the men.

"Sir, begging your pardon, but the Yankees wouldn't attack in this mess, would they?" asked one dripping picket.

Gleig forced himself to be every inch the officer. "To be sure they might," he replied stiffly, although he really didn't believe it himself.

Next day, the British force had its first skirmish with the American troops. It took place in a deep forest a few miles below the town of Nottingham, and it was Gleig's company—consisting of three officers and fifty-three men—which made first contact with the Yankees. In that area the trees grew thickly, with tangled underbrush, and the weeds and grasses were hip-high, making maneuver difficult.

The company had paused for its noonday meal when one of the corporals saw a sudden flash of light in the heavy growth to the right of the company's position. The captain went forward a few hundred feet to look, and returned with the news that there was an American force ahead, concealed in the deep woods.

Logically, the British force should have tried to creep up on the Yankees unobserved, but the captain acted as if his company was maneuvering on a European battlefield. A bugle sounded the alarm, and the company charged through the tangled woods, the men tripping and falling as they went and making enough noise to be heard in Washington.

72

At a range of about two hundred yards, the Americans opened fire. It seemed to Gleig to be a substantial force—perhaps one hundred and fifty men—and the firing was thunderous. The British pushed on more slowly, taking cover whenever possible, and firing as opportunity offered. And then, suddenly, the Americans took to their heels, seeming to disappear immediately in the dense woods.

The British company struggled a few hundred yards in pursuit, but could not catch up with the fleeing Yanks. Stopping to regroup, the British found that American marksmanship had made a miserable showing; not an Englishman had suffered so much as a scratch. The American loss was one dead—Gleig found the body propped against an oak tree.

The sweating and exultant British caught another glimpse of the American skirmishers as they reached the edge of the woods and followed the river up toward the open country around Nottingham. General Ross himself led a charge of five mounted officers against their rear, seeking to cut off their stragglers. But the stragglers struck off into the woods on either side and got away.

Gleig and his company were surprised to see other officers on horseback, since the army had started off from Benedict with only one mount. The explanation, they learned, was that patrols had been sent out to round up every horse in the neighborhood, and during the morning's march they had come up with a dozen animals. By the time the army reached the outskirts of Washington, it would have picked up more than fifty horses, some of them farm plugs without saddles.

The British found Nottingham to be a village consisting of four short streets, two running parallel with the river and two others crossing them at right angles. They also discovered that Commodore Barney and his gunboats had fled upriver a few hours before their arrival.

Gleig was content. He and some other officers billeted themselves in a cozy tobacco barn and settled down for the night. Gleig's Portuguese boy went foraging with some of the other servants and they returned with several turkeys and geese. Meanwhile, the quartermaster had issued a double allowance of bread and rum. His belly full, Gleig lay happily on a mattress made of tobacco leaves and covered himself with his cloak.

The young lieutenant would not have been so smug had he known that the invaders had missed a chance to take a most important prisoner. Secretary of State Monroe had moved ahead of the British as they marched out of Benedict, and had kept them under observation as they made their tortuous way through the humid woods and along the sandy road to Nottingham.

Monroe was in Nottingham when the fleeing American skirmishers hustled through the village, and he had tried to get them to stop and pepper the British from the houses.

A dozen riflemen clustered around Monroe to hear his proposition, but they were not enthusiastic. Monroe told them that they and some of their fellows might expect to delay the invaders for a couple of hours if their sharpshooting was efficient.

"Who are you?" one of the Americans asked the Secretary of State. Monroe identified himself. "Are you with the army?" the man asked. Monroe replied that he was a civilian official and had no connection with the military.

"Then I don't know what you're doing here, giving orders," the man told him. "We're getting out."

The skirmishers left, but Monroe stayed on and was still in

Nottingham when the first few men of the British advance entered the other end of town. He stayed long enough to have a good look, then clattered out of town without anyone's having been aware of his presence.

President Madison, surrounded by incompetents in the capital city, had reason to be proud of the conscientious daring shown by his fellow Virginian during those first two days of the British advance.

[VI]

Compromise City

ASSUREDLY, as General Armstrong was wont to complain, it was a shrewd political compromise which had ultimately located the capital city along the shores of the Potomac, but it was something far more serious than mere partisan considerations which had originally alerted Congress to the necessity of establishing a Federal city: the solid democratic premise that those who make the laws should be secured from intimidation. This fact of governmental life was borne in on

76

Congress during an era of triumph that was yet tinged with deep gloom; it was in June 1783, when Congress was sitting in Philadelphia.

Victory over England had been achieved in the War of the Revolution, but the young nation's unity was a weak and fragile thing. The Treasury was empty and the Confederacy had no credit. The colonies were free but not yet one nation; instead they were thirteen independent sovereignties quarreling with one another. Worst of all, the Treasury was heavily in debt to its soldiers for back pay, and to the separate states for money loaned to carry on the war.

It was the soldiers who pressed the issue. On the morning of June 19, a courier arrived with menacing news. A detachment of the unpaid soldiers, encamped at Lancaster, Pennsylvania, was marching to Philadelphia to demand its pay from Congress. The legislators appealed to the Executive Council of Pennsylvania for protection, but the Council insisted the state militia could not be relied on.

"A fine thing," muttered Massachusetts' Elbridge Gerry. "If this city will not support Congress, it is high time the Congress remove to some other place."

The next day the mutineers entered Philadelphia, officered by their sergeants, and for two days they held Congress in a state of siege with what was probably the first picket line in the national history. The soldiers formed a cordon around the hall where Congress was meeting and occasionally relieved their boredom by poking the muzzles of their muskets in the windows.

On the night of the second day, the soldiers were persuaded to let the legislators retire to their homes, and next morning the picket line was discontinued. But the mutineers remained in the city three more days, swaggering about the streets and threatening anybody who looked as if he might be a politician.

Congress was outraged. As Elbridge Gerry acidly put it: "We must decide whether or not the gentlemen in the Congress shall be the prisoners of the military." In taverns and in exquisite Philadelphia drawing rooms, the lawmakers wondered aloud whether a military dictatorship was about to take over the nation.

With the Philadelphia atmosphere intolerable, the Congress finally adjourned to Princeton, New Jersey, where the members debated the dangers of an undisciplined army and an unprotected Congress. No action was taken immediately, but in October of the same year Elbridge Gerry offered a resolution. It moved that buildings for the use of Congress be erected on or near the banks of the Delaware or Potomac rivers and that this cluster of government structures be incorporated into a Federal city under the exclusive jurisdiction of the Congress. At its next session, the following October, Congress appointed three commissioners to lay out a district on either bank of the Delaware.

"Not while I breathe, they won't," snapped Virginia's Thomas Jefferson. "The Potomac's the place."

Then followed nearly six years of pulling and hauling. The Southern members opposed the Delaware site on the grounds that it was not a center of population and that it would be dominated by Northern ideas and the money power of the New York and Philadelphia merchants. They plumped for the Potomac which, they argued, was not only a geographical center but would one day be the door through which the products of the West would find their way to the sea.

Jefferson and Madison led the Southern fight. They pointed

out that they already had projected a Chesapeake and Ohio canal and a national road which would plunge into the Alleghenies at the passes created by the Potomac. The Northerners listened politely and then cast the votes which kept the original resolution intact.

Still the matter remained unresolved, due largely to the influence of Washington and Jefferson, who argued and flattered the commissioners into doing nothing. In 1787, the newly adopted Constitution decreed that Congress was given exclusive power "over such district not exceeding ten miles square, as may at the cession of particular States and the acceptance of Congress become the seat of government of the United States. . . ." The section passed without debate, but two years elapsed before any action was taken on it.

The first Congress to meet under the new Constitution convened in New York in 1789 to find itself flooded with petitions for the location of the Federal city. Again the Southerners were the principal agitators. New York and New England felt there were more important matters to argue—for instance, the proposition that the Federal government assume the war debts of the states. The Northerners felt a deep interest in this because they had shouldered the biggest burden of the war and they sought due recompense.

Pennsylvania favored Wright's Ferry, on the Susquehanna, near Havre de Grace. The North united on this proposition and it passed the House, 31 to 19. In the Senate, the measure was amended by striking out the word Susquehanna and inserting a clause locating the Federal district at Germantown, near Philadelphia, provided Pennsylvania or her private citizens agreed to pay $100,000 for the erection of the necessary government buildings. The House in turn added an amendment that the laws of Pennsylvania should remain in force in the district until repealed by Congress. This amendment sent the bill back to the Senate, and since the Senate adjourned without acting on it, the measure died.

The South took advantage of the opportunity. That winter Virginia passed a law offering ten square miles of her territory on the Potomac River for the Federal city, and the sum of $120,000 for buildings. Maryland offered ten miles on its side of the Potomac and $72,000.

Immediately, the Middle Atlantic states entered the bidding. Baltimore agreed to erect every building needed for the government city. New Jersey offered to provide suitable buildings at Trenton. New York and Philadelphia pointed to the "elegant and convenient accommodations" available in their communities.

In the midst of this bidding, Congress convened in Philadelphia in 1790 and the Southerners quickly put forth their proposition of a Federal city site "on the River Potomac between the mouth of the Eastern Branch and the Conogocheague. . . ."

In a chance meeting between Secretary of the Treasury Alexander Hamilton, leader of the Northern bloc, and Secretary of State Jefferson, chief of the Southern bloc, Hamilton complained to the latter: "This cannot go on. I fear the debate on this measure threatens the dissolution of the Union. Already, the Eastern states are threatening secession."

Jefferson agreed. He was particularly disturbed that Northern and Southern members of Congress were so embittered they would not meet together for the transaction of business. He asked Hamilton to dine with him at his home the next evening "and bring one or two friends."

Hamilton showed up at dinner with Robert Morris, the Philadelphia banker who had helped to finance the Revolution. Madison was there with Jefferson. And a compromise was arranged whereby the capital would be built on the Potomac and Congress would pass a funding act permitting the Federal government to assume $21,000,000 in states' debts.

On July 10, 1790—seven years after the mutineers laid siege to Congress in Philadelphia—the bill establishing the capital of the United States became law.

The Act of Congress establishing a Federal city played an interesting trick on President Washington, who was entrusted the task of selecting the exact site and appointing the three commissioners to build the city. It was contained in the following passage: "That for defraying the expense of such purchases and buildings the President of the United States be authorized and requested to accept grants of land and money."

In other words, not a penny was appropriated by Congress for building the new city. For the time being, all Washington had to work with was the $192,000 granted by Virginia and Maryland. But the President was enthusiastic about the project and he went to work.

By early September of 1790, he had picked his site—with the help and advice of Jefferson, Madison and the famous Charles Carroll of Carrollton. It was the V-shaped green plain between the Potomac and the East Branch which merged into the blue, wooded hills of Maryland. The hills swept in a semicircle from one river to the other, and on the Potomac ended in high bluffs. Below these bluffs Scottish immigrants in 1695 had established a trading port known as Georgetown, which by 1790 was doing a lucrative business with London, Liverpool and the West Indies.

Opponents of the site had indulged in political hyperbole in describing the site as a "wilderness." It was, in fact, covered with large tobacco plantations, where the owners lived like English country gentlemen. Besides Georgetown, there were in the area two other thriving port towns—Alexandria, or Bellhaven, on the Virginia bank, and Bladensburg, six miles up the Eastern Branch.

Even in 1790, the neighborhood had a history. In 1624, only four years after the Pilgrims landed at Plymouth Rock, an English fur trader named Henry Fleet had become the first white man to look upon the land. Fleet had come to trade with the Anacostian Indians, and his journal sang the praises of the area where the new capital was about to rise.

"This place without question is the most pleasant and healthful place in all this country . . . the air temperate in summer and not violent in winter," Fleet wrote. He found the rivers abounding in fish and the forests in deer, turkeys, buffaloes and bears.

Lord Baltimore's Catholic colony had settled in Maryland in 1634, and sixty years later the entire extent of the new Federal city had been settled by Scottish and English exiles attached to the House of Stuart. Prince George's County, from which most of the capital's territory came, had been established in 1700.

With plantations covering so much of the new district, the planters had to be recompensed for the land taken. Most of the negotiations were carried on in a patrician Georgetown tavern named "Suters," a long-roofed, wide-porched structure on the post road to Bladensburg. There, night after night, Washington sat with the planters and the three commissioners—General Thomas Johnson and Daniel Carroll of Maryland, and Dr. David Stuart of Virginia. These negotiations continued throughout most of the winter of 1790-91, and when they concluded toward the close of February, Washington wrote Jefferson of the settlement made:

"The terms entered into by me on the part of the United States with the landholders of Georgetown and Carrollsburg are, that all the land from Rock Creek along the river to the Eastern Branch, and so upward to or above the ferry, including a breadth of about a mile and a half, the whole containing from three thousand to five thousand acres, is ceded to the public on condition that when the whole is laid off as a city (which Major L'Enfant is now directed to do) the present proprietors shall retain every other lot; and for such parts of the land as may be taken for public use for squares, walks, etc., they shall be allowed at the rate of twenty-five pounds an acre. Nothing to be allowed for the ground which may be occupied for streets and alleys."

Jefferson was delighted. He replied: "The acquisition of ground at Georgetown is really noble, considering that only twenty-five pounds an acre is to be paid for any ground taken for the public, and the streets not to be counted, which will, in fact, reduce it to about nineteen pounds an acre. I think very liberal reserves should be made for the public."

With the city's site secured, Washington was ready with the man to lay out the new capital. He was a middle-aged French engineer, Major Pierre Charles L'Enfant, who had served with Washington's army during the Revolution. Washington had been impressed with L'Enfant's competence in planning and rearing fortifications and had promoted him to major in the engineers.

After the war, L'Enfant had remodeled and refurbished the City Hall in New York for the use of the first Congress, and later he renovated the Federal House in Philadelphia. He was a temperamental man, subject to fits of temper and possessed of a highly developed persecution complex, but Washington recognized his genius and engaged him to draw up the necessary plans.

L'Enfant was exhilarated by this challenge. His mind was filled with grandiose, but practical, thoughts. And he looked far ahead into a future few statesmen could see. He decided to plan not for thirteen states and three million people, but for a republic of fifty states and five hundred million people.

From a boat on the Potomac, from the heights of Georgetown and from the hills of Maryland, L'Enfant studied the physical characteristics of the site. He thought of Paris' broad boulevards, and the charm and grace of Venice, Florence, London and Amsterdam—and decided that the capital of the new United States would be gracefully unique.

He took as his center an eminence in the northeast section of the district where the Capitol building would be erected, and laid down the streets parallel to it and running east and west, named alphabetically. Then he drew another set of streets, running from north to south, which he designated by figures. Finally, radiating from the capitol-to-be, he laid out a series of wide and straight avenues, cutting the checkerboard of alphebetical and numbered streets at all sorts of angles, and creating a series of squares and circles which the soldier in him reckoned would be valuable in the city's defense.

The avenues were planned to be 130 to 160 feet wide, and the streets a minimum of 90 feet wide. There were provisions for gardens and parks, and originally L'Enfant planned to extend the Capitol grounds and those of the President's Mansion to the Potomac. His city extended from northwest to southeast about four and a half miles, and from east to southwest about two and a half miles, consisting of 7,100 acres. There were to be 65 miles of avenues and 197 miles of streets; it would be a drive of 14 miles around the city.

With L'Enfant's plan in hand, the commissioners met in Georgetown on September 8 and 9, 1791, to name both the district and the city. The choices were unanimous—Columbia for the district, after Christopher Columbus, and Washington for the city, after the father of the country. The commissioners demanded the plan in order to have it engraved and published. L'Enfant refused to hand it over on the ground that publication would encourage speculators to gobble up the best locations.

The commissioners argued with L'Enfant, but when he stood firm they reported his recalcitrance to Washington. Reluctantly, on March 1, 1792, the President dismissed L'Enfant, appending to the dismissal notice a letter to the commissioners in which he commented on living with a genius:

"Men who possess talents which fit them for peculiar purposes are almost invariably under the influence of untoward dispositions, or a sottish pride, or possessed of some other disqualification by which they plague all those with whom they are concerned; but I did not expect to meet with such perverseness in Major L'Enfant as his late conduct exhibited."

Washington appointed in L'Enfant's place one Andrew Ellicott, who had surveyed the new district. Ellicott drew up a plan
virtually identical with L'Enfant's and it was published late in
1792. Meanwhile, the commissioners ordered their bankers to
place five hundred guineas at L'Enfant's disposal and wrote
him that they had also assigned him a building lot "near the
President's house."

The proud Frenchman rejected both forms of compensation,
penning a letter to the commissioners in which he begged them
to "call back your order for the money and not take any further
trouble about the lot." He returned to Philadelphia and resumed
his architectural work; and in 1812 he declined an appointment
by President Madison as Professor of Engineering at West
Point.

By March 1792, the commissioners could advertise "A pre-
mium of a lot in this city . . . and five hundred dollars . . .
will be given by the Commissioners of the Federal Buildings to
the person who before the 15th of July, 1792, shall produce to
them the most approved plan for a Capitol . . ." Shortly thereafter, they advertised for plans for a "President's House."

Only two of the many designs submitted for the Capitol were
considered seriously. One came from Dr. William Thornton of
Georgetown, an Englishman of Renaissance talents; the other
from a French architect named Étienne Sulpice Hallet, who
lived in New York. Thornton was not an architect, but he
had spent weeks reading books on the subject, and his design
impressed Washington with its "Grandeur, Simplicity and
Beauty."

The commissioners also liked Thornton's design, especially
his idea of a rotunda and two wings. But Hallet pointed out

grave mechanical defects in the plan, whereupon the commissioners rejected Thornton's design but instructed Hallet to draft the Englishman's ideas into his drawings. Hallet and Thornton subsequently were awarded identical prizes of $500 and a capital building lot.

Shortly thereafter, the commissioners accepted a design submitted for a "President's Castle" by the Irish architect James Hoban. The plan called for a modified Georgian residence of four stories, with columned porticoes at north and south entrances. The location selected was on the outskirts of Georgetown, a mile down Pennsylvania Avenue from the Capitol.

There was agitation to have the Capitol and President's Castle built of brick, in the Philadelphia fashion. But Washington and the commissioners wanted these buildings to be different, and at the same time to be representative of the country's natural resources. They decided on Virginia sandstone from quarries recently opened at Acquia Creek; there is little doubt that some of the President's friends influenced him in this decision.

Soon the site of the new capital resembled a huge open-air workshop. Long lines of teams drew blocks of stone from the river landing, and imported Scotch, French and Italian stonecutters worked on them under tentlike booths. For common labor, the commissioners hired slaves, paying wages to their owners at the rate of six dollars a month.

Scraping up the money to pay these workmen was a harassing chore. The $120,000 given by Virginia and the $72,000 voted by Maryland were soon exhausted, and money obtained by the sale of city lots failed to make up the deficit. Lotteries raised only an indifferent sum, and the commissioners were unsuccessful in their efforts to borrow from France and Holland.

Finally President Washington applied personally to the state of Maryland for a loan of $100,000. The loan was granted, but only after the commissioners agreed to be personally responsible for its repayment.

Both Congress and the President—by then the acerbic John Adams—moved into their new homes in 1800. Both buildings were unfinished at the time. Now, fourteen years later, the still new buildings were marked for destruction by an invader only thirty-eight miles away.

[VII]

Dolly's Palace

ADMIRAL COCKBURN had been hoping all along that circumstances would make a descent on Washington feasible, and was glad that this hope was about to be fulfilled. Ross still believed that the decision was a gamble—although a good one. He feared Washington might be reinforced by Virginia cavalry, which would make the British raid risky, and for that reason he was anxious to retain his present advantage by moving in quickly before the Virginians could arrive. Cockburn was more than confident however, and impatient to get a look at the notorious "President's Castle."

"We'll go through the Yankees like a physic," he told Ross.

During the Chesapeake raids, the admiral had often expressed a desire to be among the guests in "Mistress Madison's drawing room," and in this respect his curiosity was shared by the British public. Most Englishmen were amused by or contemptuous of their former colonies' presumption in building a palace for a man who bore the antiregal title of "President." British newspapers often spoke jokingly about it and sometimes wondered what disposition would be made of the house when the colonies returned to the fold of the British Empire.

By now, however, most Americans were certain of the permanence of their Presidents' home. After all, it had been occupied for nearly fourteen years, and the Madisons were its third tenants. It was beginning to have a history.

Jefferson had changed it from a crudely equipped, unfurnished and unfinished structure into an impressive residence, and now Dolly Madison had transformed it into an authentic mansion which had become the center of all social and diplomatic events. Dolly's personal charm had won the people's confidence and affection for the white sandstone "castle," although its first mistress—the tight-lipped New Englander Abigail Adams—had done much to inspire the reverse.

Arriving in Washington in November 1800, Mrs. Adams had been dismayed to discover that not a single room in the house had been finished, and that fires had to be built in thirteen separate fireplaces to dry out the freshly plastered walls.

Mrs. Adams had been impressed only by the size of the mansion—"twice as large as our meeting house," she wrote her sister. But—"The lighting of the apartments from the kitchen to parlors and chambers is a tax indeed," and she complained that there were no bells to summon servants and that it was difficult to obtain firewood.

"Surrounded with forests, can you believe that wood is not to be had, because people cannot be found to cut and cart it! Briesler entered into a contract with a man to supply him with wood; a small part, a few cords only, has he been able to get. He has had recourse to coals, but we cannot get grates made and set. We have indeed come into a *new country*."

Fresh from the neat enclosures of Boston and Philadelphia, Mrs. Adams also was annoyed to find there was "not the least fence, yard, or other convenience without." She surmounted the lack of clothes lines by hanging her washing in the "great unfinished audience room," which one day would be famous as the East Room. She never was satisfied with the rickety outdoor privies, and it displeased her so intensely to have the local citizenry wandering about the House's grounds that she absolutely insisted that a fence be built. She got her fence, a crude rail affair, and a stable, even though her projected stay at the President's House would be for only four months, since her husband had been defeated for re-election by Jefferson's new Republican party several weeks before she had moved to Washington.

So it was that the President's House toward which the British invaders turned their thoughts in August 1814 was largely the result of Jefferson's determination to create a residence of "some grace" from this "great barn." Jefferson brought to the job imagination, a flair for architecture and interior decoration, and unceasing and painstaking labor.

When the house was being built, Jefferson had worked closely with Washington and the architect Hoban, and many of Jefferson's ideas had been incorporated in Hoban's plans. Installed in the mansion as President in March 1801, Jefferson brought to the infant city the brilliant architect and engineer Benjamin Henry Latrobe, whom he appointed Surveyor of Public Buildings at $1,700 a year. Mostly, he wanted Latrobe's guidance on how to improve the President's House.

Jefferson trusted Latrobe; that is to say, he was aware that Latrobe's ideas were similar to his own, including a penchant for the classic. Jefferson was almost fanatic in this regard. He saw his country in the ideas and traditions of the young French Republic, and believed the United States should discard the elaborate styles of the Renaissance and adopt the classic styles which would symbolize Republican democracy.

With Jefferson at his elbow, Latrobe redesigned the south portico to give it a broad flight of steps, in place of the lighter piazza drafted by Hoban. He also revised the design for the north portico, facing Pennsylvania Avenue, giving it its series of beautiful rising columns and dressing it up with a flight of stone steps and a stone landing.

Where Hoban's plan called for wings on the east and west, Jefferson built long, low terraces similar to the servants' wings in Monticello, with colonnades facing south. The upper part of the terraces served as covered promenades, while within were rooms for storage of fuel and provisions which had been overlooked in the original plan. To the west, Jefferson built himself a small office.

Jefferson and Latrobe also landscaped the grounds. Large sections were leveled off, and trees and shrubs were planted.

Abigail Adams' rail fence was replaced with a low stone coping which was inadequate for keeping idlers off the grounds but which Latrobe argued was more dignified than a "farmer's fence." As a farmer himself, Jefferson thought that over for a while before approving it.

After Latrobe had supervised the repair of several bedrooms in which the plaster was falling, Jefferson furnished twenty-three rooms. Some of the furniture was his own, from Monticello; the rest was bought by a reluctant Congress. By the time Ross and Cockburn had landed at Benedict, the house was almost fully furnished.

The style was varied—Sheraton, Hepplewhite, Adams, the French Louis Quinze and Seize and Directoire. Much of it was gilded. Jefferson introduced cotton for draperies in the state rooms, and painted canvas covered all but the most important floors, including the great entrance hall. There was an amazing number of chairs: twenty-eight in the entrance hall, all with haircloth covers, thirty-four black-and-gold armchairs in the East Room, and about twelve gold-and-damask chairs per bedroom.

It was Jefferson who installed the famous "gadgets" which now so fascinated Dolly Madison. One of them was in the Green Room, which he used as a small dining room. It was a set of circular shelves, really a mechanical lazy Susan. The shelves were set in the wall so that when a spring was touched they revolved slowly into the pantry where the servants loaded them with food.

Jefferson also had a little cabinet in one of the parlors where he often worked late. This opened with a spring to disclose the President's midnight snack—a goblet of water, a decanter of wine and a plate of light cakes. In that way, Jefferson explained, he avoided keeping a servant up to wait on him. And in his bedroom he built a turnstile-like contrivance on which he hung his jackets and breeches so he could readily select his day's apparel.

Washington was Jefferson's dream city, and there were reasons other than the aesthetic which caused him to spend so much time giving the President's House its look of elegant permanence. The capital was still in such disorder, with its mud holes and blackened tree stumps, that there was considerable agitation to move the government to another location. Jefferson was determined to preserve the Federal city.

Newspapers in New York and Philadelphia were forever gibing at Washington as "the village in the wilderness," calling attention to "the puddles under the skylights" in the Capitol and the miserable, bug-ridden boardinghouses provided for members of Congress. It was a city, they said, where "men of talent were expected to expatriate themselves for six months in the year, deprived of the society of wives and children, and of the comforts of civilized life." They maintained that an Eastern city would be a far more suitable location for the nation's capital.

By March 1804, a bill to remove the seat of government to Baltimore passed to its second reading in the Senate. Another bill was offered in the House to re-cede the District back to Maryland and Virginia, on the grounds that Congress spent too much time enacting the legislation necessary to govern its new domain. But Jefferson and his Virginia friends—with help from some of the new Western Congressmen who distrusted the money interests of New York and Philadelphia—managed to kill these alternative proposals.

Jefferson, a widower for eighteen years, had two married

daughters who paid him occasional visits. But they both had growing families and Jefferson refused to let them leave their homes for any long period of time. As the wife of his Secretary of State, close friend and political confidant in the new Republican party, Dolly Madison was Jefferson's obvious choice to preside over the weekly state dinners, and the huge receptions which Jefferson filled with as many "average citizens" as he could persuade to attend. Thus Dolly had begun to add her feminine touch to the President's House long before her husband became its elected occupant.

Christened Dorothy, Dolly Madison was a widow of twenty-six when Madison, then a forty-three-year-old Congressman, first became attracted to her. After her husband, John Todd, had died during the yellow fever epidemic in Philadelphia in 1793, she had moved back to her mother's boardinghouse in that same city.

During the rest of that year, Madison often saw the attractive widow attending to chores. Although he was socially reticent by nature, he was most direct in this one instance. He went to Aaron Burr, then a Senator from New York, and asked Burr to make the necessary introduction.

At the time, there were rumors that Burr himself was interested in Dolly Payne Todd. Burr's wife had died recently, and he was known as a good friend and business adviser to the newly widowed Mrs. Todd. But Madison had gone to President Washington to ask that Burr, the choice of a party caucus, be appointed Minister to France. Burr had set his heart on the appointment, and he needed friends because Washington was reluctant to name him to the post.

Burr therefore set aside whatever romantic notions of his

own he might have held, and sent along a note to Dolly Todd. She was surprised and pleased at its contents, and immediately wrote to her close friend Elizabeth Collins: "Thou must come to me—Aaron Burr says that the great little Madison has asked to be brought to see me this evening."

The courtship lasted four months. James Madison and Dolly Payne Todd were married on September 15, 1794, at Harewood, the Virginia plantation of George Steptoe Washington, nephew and namesake of the President, and husband of Dolly's sister Lucy. But Burr did not reap his own hoped-for reward; he remained seated in the Senate while Washington appointed James Monroe Ambassador to France.

The Madisons arrived in Washington in the family carriage from Montpelier on May 1, 1801. With them was Dolly's son, nine-year-old Payne Todd, and Dolly's sister, the eligible Anna Payne, who soon became Mrs. Richard Cutts, wife of the Massachusetts congressman.

Madison was sworn in the next day as Secretary of State, and after the ceremony President Jefferson at once asked Mrs. Madison to take over as his official hostess, and pressed his new Cabinet member to accept his personal hospitality in the President's House. He reminded Madison that houses were scarce in Washington—real estate speculators had shown surprising moderation—and that he was living alone in a mansion large enough to house a dozen families.

Little Jemmy Madison agreed with some reluctance to move his family into the President's House. He told Jefferson that he feared "what people will say when they hear the Secretary of State is living in a house maintained by public monies." Besides, he wanted to settle down in a neat home of his own; the tough little man was uncomfortable unless he was master of his own ménage.

Finding a house took time, however. Jefferson suggested that Madison buy one of the new brick houses near the President's, but Madison was afraid its value would soar and he would be accused of speculation. It was several weeks before the Madisons found a small house on M Street near Thirty-second, in Georgetown. It was inadequate, but Madison felt bound to take it; political enemies were already joking about Jefferson "taking in boarders."

Happily, the energetic Dr. William Thornton, architect of the Capitol, then stepped in and started hunting for a more suitable home for the Madisons. The Secretary of State and Dolly had known the Thorntons slightly in Philadelphia; moreover Thornton was a close friend of Jefferson's.

Thornton got the job done. He wrote Madison in Montpelier in August: "My dear Friend: I accordingly turned my attention to Mr. Voss's House next door to the one I occupy; but was afraid we should not agree. We have, however, concluded; but I was under the necessity of infringing one of the rules not really specified but strongly hinted in your letters.

"I was obliged to agree to an advance of the rent on your entering the House, but laid him under a penalty of $1,000 Dollars if the House should not be finished by the 1st of October. The cellar I have directed to be divided, that one may serve for Wine etc., the other for Coals, etc.—and for security against Fire a cupola on the roof which will add to the House in other respects."

Both James and Dolly Madison were delighted with Nicholas Voss's house at 1333 F Street, next door to the Thorntons.

They moved in in the fall and Madison was pleased to note that Thornton had anticipated many of the features he himself had thought of.

The Madisons lived in the F Street house throughout Madison's tenure as Secretary of State. There they formed their lasting friendship with the Thorntons, an amiable, intelligent couple. Thornton was a staunch Federalist whose talents nevertheless had been recognized by the Republican Jefferson, who had named him a District Commissioner. He and Madison ignored their differing politics to enjoy each other's company, and made a little money on their joint ownership of the race horse, Wild Medley. Thornton was one of the few men whom Madison felt he could trust and with whom he could unbend enough to tell one of his infrequent risqué stories. Later, when Madison became President, he appointed Thornton Superintendent of Patents.

Dolly Madison, with her easy, outgoing charm, found a congenial companion in the more acidulous Mrs. Thornton, despite their different temperaments. They visited together for tea almost every day, borrowed each other's servants for big dinner parties, and often went sight-seeing in the half-finished city. When the Madisons moved into the White House as its official tenants, Mrs. Thornton apparently feared the intimacy between the two families would end. She wrote in her diary: "We bought Mr. Madison's dining table for $50. Mr. and Mrs. Madison dined with us for the last time, I suppose."

Mrs. Thornton was wrong. On March 11, 1809, she made note that "Mr. and Mrs. Madison went to the *Great House*, Mr. M. came in after dinner for a few minutes." Shortly thereafter an entry shows that the Thorntons "dined at the President's with a large party," and on June 26, 1809, Mrs. Thornton's diary reports: "Therm. 90°. Got ice from the President's."

During this time, Dolly Madison was doing the shopping and general managing which imposed her personality even more thoroughly on the President's House, already bearing her impress from Jefferson's reign. For the Oval Drawing Room, later renamed the Blue Room, Dolly bought new sofas and high-backed chairs and had them upholstered in sunflower-yellow satin to go with her damask draperies. She replaced many of Jefferson's chairs and did over several rooms in lighter colors. She also installed the servants' bells that Abigail Adams had lacked, and bought a new rug for the drawing room; when it arrived she thriftily sent the old one up to the House of Representatives.

When food costs rose as a result of the unpopular war with England—the price of a turkey had soared to seventy-five cents, a whole pig was all of three dollars, and potatoes were up to forty cents a bushel—some of the ordinary folk were inclined to attribute this inflation to the money Dolly had spent installing the large mirrors and damask drapes in her "Oval Parlor."

Nonetheless, the plain citizen was also willing to abide Dolly—the onetime Quaker widow—because of her winning charm and easygoing habits. The people enjoyed meeting her at the markets, where Dolly often went to stock her larder, and they liked the stories of her down-to-earth gaiety at the parties in the Mansion.

In particular, Washington savored the story of the night Dolly offered Kentucky's Congressman Henry Clay a helping from her lava snuff box. When both had had a dip, she fished out from a deep pocket in her dress a huge bandanna and after plying it vigorously tucked it out of sight and flourished a dainty white lace handerchief. She explained prettily that the bandanna was "for heavy work only," while the lacy square was her "polisher."

Dolly's charm clearly had its effect on Congress as well. Shortly after the Madisons moved into the Executive Mansion, the legislators ordered Secretary of the Treasury Gallatin to release $6,000 "to finish and decorate" its interior. Dolly handed the job over to Benjamin Latrobe, and that genial architect spent much of his time running back and forth to Philadelphia, Baltimore and New York in search of furniture and materials.

Among other things, Latrobe and Dolly bought a pianoforte for $458 and a guitar for $28. Table linen and a "looking glass" cost another $1,225 and new china $556.15. Latrobe won a notable victory when he persuaded Dolly to hang the portrait of George Washington in the dining room. She had wanted it in the drawing room, but Latrobe insisted that "the dining room is properly the picture room."

He also won Dolly over to a state carriage of reddish brown trimmed inside with yellow lace. Dolly had wanted a black coach with red interior. Latrobe pointed out that black was too common and, besides, "it is much too somber for a lady of your cheerful disposition."

One young visitor to the President's House found that the "cheerful" Dolly had created a setting that was not only "cheerful" but truly magnificent, although this elegant edifice still had no running water or sewerage. Elbridge Gerry, dapper son of Madison's Vice President, wrote impressively to his friend:

"The President's House is a perfect palace. You enter the front door and are at once in a large hall. . . Pillars of immense size are dispersed thro' this and it has large lamps for the whole length. On the side opposite to the entrance are doors opening to four rooms. The corner is the dining room and is very spacious, and twice the height of modern parlors and three times as large. This is furnished in the most elegant manner, and the furniture is so large the sideboard would cover the whole side of a large parlor. At the head of the room George Washington is represented as large as life.

"This room opens by a single door into Mrs. Madison's sitting-room which is half as large. This is furnished equally as well and has more elegant and delicate furniture. Her portrait is here seen. This room, in the same way, enters into the drawing-room, which is an immense and magnificent room, in an oval form, and which form is preserved in those above and even to the cellar. A door opens at each end, one into the hall, an opposite one into the terrace, from whence you have an elegant view of all the rivers, etc. The windows are nearly the height of the room and the curtains cost $4.00 a yard. The chairs are wood painted with worked bottoms and each has a red velvet large cushion. They are arranged on the side and are divided into four divisions by sofas."

In the new elegance of the President's House, Dolly Madison entertained on a lavish scale. Although some disgruntled Federalists muttered at Mrs. Madison's extravagance in employing thirty servants, even such a large corps of domestics was not adequate to Dolly's demands. When she gave one of her large dinners she hired extra waiters at thirty-five cents for the evening to make sure each guest had his own. And her Wednesday evening levees became famous all over the country.

On such occasions, Dolly always entered the drawing room promptly, usually with a book in one hand.

A guest once wondered how she found time to read, with so many duties pressing on her. Dolly was charmingly candid.

"Oh, I always read a lot at Montpelier," she told him, "but I don't read a word here. I have this book in my hand—a very fine copy of *Don Quixote*—to have something not ungraceful to say and, if need be, to supply a word of talk."

Madison moved about abstractedly at these affairs, his countenance pallid and a trifle grim, and seldom uttered anything but the formalities. It was not until most of the guests had left and he was surrounded by old friends that he relaxed, exchanged stories and became, as one guest put it, "almost facetious."

At the dinner parties in the President's House, Dolly sat at the head of the table, with Madison at the side. "It relieves him of the necessity of leading the conversation," Dolly told Mrs. Thornton. "He would much rather listen." And Dolly, of course, loved to talk.

Dolly always dressed herself with elegance for these soirees. One of her favorite outfits was a robe of plain light-blue satin, trimmed with ermine, topped by a white velvet-and-satin turban with nodding ostrich plumes. On her tiny feet she wore evening shoes from Paris that were the envy of all the ladies. Dolly had a dozen pairs of these slippers, some of gold and silver and blue satin and others heavily beaded or buckled.

Even the modest Mrs. Thornton was impressed by the number and elegance of Dolly's evening slippers. "Most ladies of our class are satisfied with three pairs," she told her husband, "but Dolly has gone the limit. I must say all her shoes are quite proper for her station, however."

Washington Irving summed up the Madisons in an article he wrote for the *New England Palladium*. He had wangled an invitation to a levee from a New York neighbor who knew Albert Gallatin, and he told about the affair in print.

"In a few minutes I emerged from dirt and darkness into the blazing splendor of Mrs. Madison's drawing-room. Here I was most graciously received; found a crowded collection of great and little men, of ugly old women and beautiful young ones, and in ten minutes was hand in glove with half the people in the assemblage.

"Mrs. Madison is a fine, portly, buxom dame, who has a smile and a pleasant word for everybody. Her sisters, Mrs. Cutts and Mrs. Washington, are like the two merry wives of Windsor; but as to Jemmy Madison—ah poor Jemmy!—he is but a withered apple-john."

But even while foreign diplomats admired Dolly's gracious hospitality at the Executive Mansion, they failed to be impressed by the capital city itself. To be sure, it had those new ice-cream parlors, and an open-air arena where *Macbeth* was produced with swallows flying overhead, and the classic simplicity of the new government buildings. But Washington in many respects remained a frontier town; there were no police and only a few broken stretches of sidewalk along Pennsylvania Avenue. There were still only three street lights—also on Pennsylvania Avenue—installed in 1801 at a cost of one hundred dollars. But since no appropriation had been made for their upkeep, they were maintained at the expense of private property owners for their own convenience. However, the crudeness of the city only further increased the citizen's pride in the splendor of the President's House.

103

But one of the residents of the house did not share in its general popularity. This was Dolly's son, Payne Todd, who was noticeably absent from the family circle and social gatherings. At first this was understandable, since the boy was away at boarding school, but later it was because Payne skipped his mother's parties to join merrier and louder companions in Washington's rough and tough taverns.

By the time of the War of 1812, Payne Todd had become a problem. He was tall and handsome and a favorite with the ladies, but he couldn't handle the position of being the President's son. Madison had wanted to send him to his own alma mater, Princeton, but Payne had refused to leave the gaiety of life in Washington for the dreary routine of scholarship. When his gambling debts mounted, he by-passed Madison and borrowed the money from Richard Cutts.

Payne served a few months in a militia regiment in 1812, but he was an indifferent soldier who was forever inventing "official" excuses to get back to the capital. Madison had finally sent word to his commanding officer that Payne was not to leave his company without written orders from the President.

Finally, in 1813, when Payne was twenty-one, the Madisons found a way to get him away from Washington's temptations. The peace commission was sailing in May for St. Petersburg, and Gallatin's son was going along with his father. Madison added Payne's name to the passenger list. Now, almost two years later, with the British perilously close to the capital, Dolly was just as glad that Payne was still away. Her husband's safety and the success of Washington's defense were subjects enough for her concern.

[VIII]

Chaos by the Campfires

By Sunday, August 21, the American Army was at Wood Yard, twelve miles to the southeast of the city, with General Winder in personal, if fitful, command. The force numbered 4,000 troops of assorted fighting quality, including Commodore Barney and 400 of his 503 seamen. The remainder had been ordered to join Winder's troops later after blowing up the gunboats as the British advanced. And additional help was on the way, as a result of Winder's repeated calls to Baltimore for assistance. General Samuel Smith, a Revolutionary War veteran who commanded the Baltimore troops, had finally dispatched 3,300 men to positions at or near Bladensburg, just over the Potomac's Eastern Branch from Washington. These included the brigade of General Tobias E. Stansbury, another Revolutionary veteran, the 5th Maryland Infantry commanded by Lieutenant Colonel Sterrett, two companies of artillery and a rifle battalion led by former Ambassador, Congressman and Attorney General William Pinkney, and a regiment of 800 men under Colonel William D. Beall, another Revolutionary soldier.

With these reinforcements, plus his own 4,000 men, Winder could anticipate command of more than 7,000 troops, which seemed more than sufficient to repulse the British. Yet he still was most apprehensive about the size of the invading army. He paid more attention to wild reports about a force of 11,000 redcoats on the march than he did to Monroe's careful estimate of no more than 6,000.

From the moment he took to the field, Winder displayed his customary lack of judgment and ability. At Wood Yard, his troops were on the left flank of Ross's army as it marched toward Upper Marlborough. Winder himself observed the marching invaders from a ridge overlooking the roadway a half-dozen miles away. Most generals would have given their right arm for such a chance to harass and delay the enemy, but Winder returned to camp and busied himself with some paper work while Ross entered Upper Marlborough unimpeded.

In that pleasant village, Ross suddenly delayed his troops of his own accord. He kept his men at ease most of Monday, August 22, while his veterans wondered at his sluggishness, and

Winder suffered from nervousness and bewilderment at his opponent's tactics.

The British general did his waiting in the hospitable home of Dr. William Beanes, a physician who was an ardent Federalist and a fanatic opponent of the war with England. Dr. Beanes provided food and drink for Ross's party and handed over several of his horses; Ross thanked him courteously and bade his commissary reimburse the American. Lieutenant Gleig was among the party and soon learned the reason for delay.

Ross knew what he was doing. He was awaiting information from his spies on the general situation in Washington, the size and quality of the defending army and an on-the-ground estimate of the best approach to the city.

James H. Blake, mayor of Washington, had done his part as best he could. On Sunday, August 21, he had posted the following notice addressed to the citizenry of the capital:

"All able-bodied Citizens remaining here and all free-men of color, are required to convene tomorrow morning at 6 o'clock precisely, at the Capitol—and from thence to proceed to a site near Bladensburg, to throw up a breastwork or redoubt, deemed important by the Commanding General, for the defense of our city. Those who cannot attend in person, will please send substitutes.

"Shovels, spades and pick-axes will be furnished on the spot.

"Each man must take his provisions for the day with him."

On the next day, August 22, the *National Intelligencer* proudly reported that "at the hour appointed, an immense crowd (supposed to amount to 4 or 5 hundred) of every description of persons, attended to offer their services. . . . It is with much pleasure also we state that on this occasion the free people of color in this city acted as became patriots . . . conducting themselves with the utmost order and propriety." No one thought it odd that this tribute should appear in the same issue which also carried an advertisement offering "Negroes for Sale."

Indeed, the *National Intelligencer's* four pages showed a curious blend of concern about the invasion and an apparent determination to retain the normal routine as long as possible.

The editor, under an article headed THE ENEMY, warned his subscribers that "Nearly all the rumors that reach us from the scene of action are evidently so exaggerated and so contradictory, that it is impossible to form from them anything like a correct or satisfactory opinion either of the strength or operations of the enemy." He did, however, offer a short letter which he said "may be confided in."

The letter reported that "The enemy's flankers (as we suppose) have advanced near the farm of Mr. Benjamin Ogden, and his main body to Upper Marlborough; his force is not exactly known but presumed to be from 5 to 6,000."

In a paragraph under this report, the *Intelligencer* asked for understanding from its readers: "In the present circumstances of this District, our readers will find a sufficient apology for the leanness of today's paper. A single object at this time occupies all hands and hearts."

Yet the paper contained many of the usual items of local interest and peacetime concern. The Richmond and Washington *Dispatch* announced a new line of stages between the two cities, leaving from one city at four A.M. one day and arriving in the other city at six P.M. the next day; seamen who had served in a Lake Erie action on September 15, 1813, were informed they could obtain their prize money aboard the *Java*, anchored off Baltimore; and T. Monroe advertised that he had lost his pet monkey, "perfectly hairy and the color of a fox." However, no one paid much attention to these extraneous notices; with the British finally on the march, Washington had become a garrison town, and everyone was occupied with personal or public defense.

Humble citizens continued to flee into the countryside and Mrs. Samuel Harrison Smith, wife of the president of the Bank of Washington and Commissioner of Revenue, kept a pistol by her side for protection against the Negroes she was sure would revolt.

With the President in and out of the city, Dolly Madison likewise armed herself—with an ancient Tunisian saber presented her by a diplomatic admirer. The foreign diplomatic colony had joined the exodus, all but M. Serurier, the French ambassador, who scurried in and out of Octagon House, a fascinated observer of the scene—and an astute gatherer of intelligence.

Before Madison rode off that morning of August 22 to participate in a series of councils of war, the gentle president had inquired anxiously, as Dolly later put it, "whether I had courage, or firmness, to remain in the President's House until his return, on the morrow, or succeeding day." Dolly assured him she had no fear "but for him and the success of our army." Madison thereupon embarked upon his mission, after asking Dolly to preserve carefully the Cabinet papers. She was left alone in charge of the House and a staff of terrified servants.

At the State Department, one S. Pleasanton began packing the State Department files in linen sacks which he had ordered the day news came of the British landing at Benedict. Pleasanton had been in the government service long enough to realize that the day-to-day business of a nation depends more on records than on men.

Dropping in from his War Department office in the same small brick building adjoining the President's House, Secretary of War Armstrong asked Pleasanton what he was doing.

"I'm going to remove these records to a safe place," Pleasanton told him.

Armstrong clucked. "It looks to me like an unnecessary alarm," he told Monroe's clerk.

But Pleasanton was not to be deterred. He got wagons and ordered the records transferred to a gristmill owned by Edgar Patterson on the Virginia side of the Chain Bridge. When he reached the mill, Pleasanton still wasn't satisfied. He sent the papers on to Leesburg, Virginia, where he rented a vacant house and there placed the papers under the custodianship of the Reverend Littlejohn, internal revenue collector for the district.

Armstrong was doing nothing about the War Department files; he insisted there was plenty of time. So Madison, prodded by Monroe, went over Armstrong's head and had the papers removed to the same Leesburg refuge. The history-conscious Monroe had pointed out that it was most important to save the original records of the Revolutionary War soldiers.

Up on Capitol Hill, there was no such efficiency as that displayed by Pleasanton. Every clerk on the staff of Patrick Magruder, Clerk of the House, had been mustered into service with the militia on August 19. It was not until two days later that an assistant named Sam Burch was furloughed by an order directing him to "return to the Capitol and save such papers as was possible."

Burch's orders added, however, that he was not to begin packing up until "the clerks at the War Office were engaged in that business." Thus Armstrong's negligence delayed the packing job at the Capitol until noon of the twenty-second.

By two o'clock of that same afternoon, Ross's spies had returned with enough information for the British commander to continue his advance. Ross penned a report to his superiors before marching off with his men:

"Having advanced within sixteen miles of Washington, and ascertained the force of the enemy to be such as might authorize an attempt to carry his capital, I determined to make it, and accordingly put the troops in movement on the evening [sic] of the 22nd."

His buglers sent the troops scurrying to their stations, and after leaving five hundred Marines and his six-pounder to protect his rear at Upper Marlborough, Ross ordered the remainder of his forces to resume their march on Washington. By now his invading army numbered 3,500 men.

It was a crucial time of decision for General Winder, and the incorrigible Marylander naturally chose the path which would delay a showdown. Instead of pushing on and attacking Ross's moving column, he ordered his army to fall back to Long Old Fields (later to become the town of Forestville, Maryland), five miles nearer Washington.

By the time Winder's disorderly troops reached their camp at Long Old Fields, the Maryland militia under General Stansbury had taken up its position at Bladensburg. Other Maryland units were expected to arrive in the Bladensburg vicinity the following day. General Winder had managed it so that he now commanded a divided force, with the Maryland militia ten miles away from the main body of American troops.

The Long Old Fields camp must have caused George Washington to groan in his grave on that night of Monday, August 22, 1814. Nobody seemed to know what was going on. Militiamen wandered about, filling the air with coarse shouting and quarrelsome phrases, and there were dozens of fist fights. The pickets were sloppy and trigger-happy; soldiers coming into the camp stopped at a safe distance to shout the countersign lest they catch a bullet from the impetuous guards.

An Alexandria recruit straggling in late, confessed to a friend, as they sat down to some salt beef and biscuit, that he had forgotten the password.

"How did you get into the camp?" asked his comrade.

"Oh, I just hung about in the woods until I heard somebody holler it out," the recruit happily replied.

These two militiamen were lucky they had something to eat. Many of the troops went hungry because, although Winder had drawn rations for 7,000 men, they were delayed in arriving because so many of the quartermaster's supply wagons were transporting government records to Virginia.

A soldier named Wolfe stole a pig from a nearby farm and was dressing it by his campfire when General Winder happened by.

"A pig!" exclaimed Winder. "Where did you get that beast?"

The soldier squirmed. Then: "It followed me, sir."

Winder rode off, shaking his head at the confusion which he himself had created.

A comparative quiet finally was restored to the camp by midnight, but two hours later, the snores of the soldiers were interrupted by the rattle of musket fire, and the whole camp woke up and groped sleepily in the dark for its weapons. It was a false alarm, but General Winder was too nervous to let it pass. The general who had been taken by surprise at Stony Creek kept the army in listless formation for the remainder of the night.

The next morning, Tuesday, August 23, the army paraded in review for President Madison, Secretary of War Armstrong, Attorney General Rush and other dignitaries who had arrived during the night. The men did their best and most of them managed to keep in step at least while passing the reviewing stand, but it was not an impressive sight. Only half the men wore uniforms and some of them were still waiting for the muskets that would arrive later in the day. Only Commodore Barney, in a neat blue uniform, and his seamen looked like professional fighting men.

For journalism, however, it was quite a historic occasion. Joseph Gales, editor of the *National Intelligencer*, was on hand to report the review for his newspaper, and thus became the first American war correspondent to accompany an American army in the field. Gales reported that the men were "all in fine spirits."

At that, the men were not in worse shape than the Cabinet officers, who had been conferring most of the night before. Indeed, Secretary of State James Monroe never showed up for the review; he had spent the night riding back and forth between the two American camps. Stopping off in Washington between liaison gallops, Monroe told the French ambassador, M. Serurier, that if a battle was to be fought it must be fought at Bladensburg, for that was the only hope of saving Washington.

President Madison had had no chance at all to stop off in Washington since his early departure from the President's House the previous morning. However, he had sent two dispatches to Dolly, the second of which had warned her to be ready to leave the city at a moment's notice. The enemy, Madison told her, was stronger than had been reported, and probably had designs on the destruction of the Capitol.

Dolly was prepared for flight. She had filled several trunks with Cabinet papers and had them loaded into a carriage. She resigned herself to sacrificing the Madisons' personal belongings because it was impossible to get wagons for their removal. Yet she waited. As she wrote her sister, Lucy Washington, in the midst of her packing, "I am determined not to go myself until I see Mr. Madison safe, and he can accompany me—as I hear of much hostility towards him."

Her own safety now seemed seriously threatened. Her husband had assigned Colonel Charles Carroll of Carrollton, reputed to be America's richest man, and a guard of one hundred militia to protect the First Lady. But the militia had joined the refugees streaming out of town and now even Colonel Carroll had mysteriously disappeared.

Still Dolly continued to wait. She drew comfort from the presence and resolution of an old and loyal factotum. This was "French John," born Jean Pierre Sioussat, who had joined the staff shortly after the Madisons moved into the President's House and who had become a combination housekeeper and social secretary to the First Lady. French John had been born in Paris and had lived his boyhood amidst the terrible events of the Reign of Terror. He had enlisted in the French Navy and then deserted by swimming ashore from his vessel as it lay in New York Harbor. French John now showed himself an activist. He came to Dolly with an aggressive proposition.

"Madame, the British surely will come here," French John told the First Lady. "We should try to see that they do not invade these premises unmolested. Let me spike the cannon at the gates and then lay a train of powder which will blow up the Englishmen should they enter this house."

Amidst the disaffection which stalked around her, Dolly was delighted with French John's audacity. But, as she wrote her sister a few minutes later, "To the last proposition I positively objected, without, however, being able to make him understand why all advantages in war may not be taken."

It was not that Dolly lacked a proper fighting spirit. Only a few days before, in a conversation with Mrs. Thornton, she had rather shocked her listener by her virulent remark—"I wish we had ten thousand men to sink our enemy to the bottomless pit."

Outside the President's House, Washington continued in a state of utter confusion. Children ran about the streets while their mothers packed belongings and sought transportation to flee the city; there were few men on the streets because most of them were under arms. A merchant wrote his law firm in New York, "I have just returned from taking a load of children eight miles out of town and the road was filled with women and children."

[IX]

Rabble on the Field

THE FAMOUS "Moore Quickstep"—three steps at a trot and three at a walk—was taking its toll of Ross's hardened troops. Citizens observing their rapid progress noted that in some cases the soldiers' mouths were open and they were gasping for breath. Many men fell from the ranks, some forever. In all, a dozen British soldiers died of sunstroke before the column reached Washington.

From time to time the redcoats were harassed by snipers but

the American sharpshooters were off their form and they were little more than a nuisance. Yet Colonel William Thornton, commanding the light brigade which was the British advance unit, had one narrow escape.

Thornton and a squad of men had overtaken one of a band of eight or ten riflemen in a wood, and the colonel was about to direct several of his men to secure the prisoner. But suddenly the American leveled his musket and fired. He missed Thornton by inches, the bullet clipping a bit of cloth off the colonel's blouse, then took advantage of the confusion to make his getaway.

Some ten miles from Washington, Ross maneuvered a feint which threw General Winder into confusion. The British commander marched his troops into the road leading to Fort Washington, just below Alexandria on the widening Potomac. But as soon as his last column had wheeled into the roadway, Ross reversed front and turned his army back and onto the road to Bladensburg. Winder, however, thought Ross was moving to outflank him, and he ordered his men to fall back to the safety of Washington.

The retreat—on the night of Tuesday, August 23—was one of the most disorderly flights in military history. It was, literally, an eight-mile run. Captains at the sides of the column hurried along the men, who were stumbling and gasping for breath after the first three miles. When they finally arrived at their camping ground at Combs, near the Eastern Branch Bridge on the outskirts of the capital city, the troops collapsed in exhaustion and it was some time before the officers could force them to take their stations and make camp.

General Winder was in a state of physical and mental exhaustion. During the retreat he had fallen off his horse and banged his shoulder and he suffered from both pain and shock. This, added to two retreats and two sleepless nights, had reduced his outlook to one of total pessimism; he was overwhelmed by a premonition of disaster.

Riding into Washington on a winded horse, the general called on Madison at the Navy Yard in southwest Washington and spent more than an hour delivering his gloomy report. Madison said afterward, "I wish I had not let the man in." Then Winder left Madison and went on to see Secretary of War Armstrong, whom he had to rouse from his bed. Armstrong was devoid of ideas; he told Winder he must make up his mind to make a stand somewhere.

En route back to camp, Winder's horse gave itself up to exhaustion and refused to take another step. Winder had to walk the rest of the way, from the west side of the Capitol, and he fell several times before finally reaching the bivouac. There, he sat down and wrote a long letter to Armstrong, pleading for guidance from the government.

"I have found it necessary to establish my headquarters here, the most advanced position convenient to the troops and nearest information," wrote Winder. "I shall remain stationary as much as possible, that I may be the more readily found, to issue orders, and collect together the various detachments of militia, and give them as rapid a consolidation and organization as possible . . . The news up the river is very threatening . . . I should be glad of the assistance of counsel from yourself and the government. If more convenient, I should make an exertion to go to you the first opportunity."

The letter was delivered by courier to Armstrong, who took

it to Madison. A council of war was called for dawn on the morning of August 24.

Meanwhile, Colonel Monroe had arrived in General Stansbury's camp in Bladensburg. Monroe had stayed on Ross's flank during the British advance and he wanted the Americans now to take aggressive action. Specifically, he wanted Stansbury to march toward Upper Marlborough and attack Ross's rear while Winder was at his front.

But Stansbury's men were dead-tired. They had been marched and countermarched for two days because Winder's false intelligence had caused him to order the Baltimore militia first to one spot, and then another, to harry the British advance. Moreover, they were almost suffocated in the winter uniforms which were the only clothing that could be found for them at the time of their recruitment. For the past few days they had been eating tainted beef and bad flour, and in one regiment 250 men were ill. They were clearly in no shape to advance.

Then, a few hours after Monroe's arrival, a sentry firing into a thicket at a mysterious noise had caused a false alarm, and the men had been formed for a night attack and were kept under arms until daylight. Stansbury had not heard of Winder's retreat to southwest Washington and did not get the news until 2 A.M., when an order from Winder directed Stansbury to "give battle to the enemy, should he appear at Bladensburg, in which case, if necessary, I will join you."

The utter inadequacy of American intelligence was reflected in the council of war Stansbury then immediately convened among his officers. They all agreed their force could not face alone a British army which they believed numbered 10,000 men, and which they thought was commanded by Lord Hill, one of Europe's most famous tacticians.

So Stansbury ordered his militia to vacate Bladenburg and, moving down the east side of the East Branch, they crossed the river and took up positions south of Bladensburg, between the East Branch and the District of Columbia line. Monroe took to the saddle again and rode into Washington to find out what was going on.

Madison's council of war at the Navy Yard was unprecedented in military history. News of the council, which consisted of Secretary Armstrong, Secretary of the Navy Jones, Secretary of the Treasury George Washington Campbell, Attorney General Rush, and General Winder, had spread about the city, and from time to time prominent citizens barged in on the session and stated their views on how the city could best be defended.

Once, when Madison sought to interrupt a particularly windy orator, the man turned to the President of the United States and said: "I beg you, sir, not to break in on my statement; it is most impolite."

About ten o'clock in the morning of August 24—with the temperature already at a sizzling 98 degrees—a platoon of Major Laval's dragoons rode up with the news that the British were moving on Bladensburg. Monroe showed up a short time later and obtained the President's permission to return to Bladensburg. Meanwhile, the council continued its deliberations, and it was not until eleven o'clock that General Winder ordered his troops to follow Monroe and make juncture with the Maryland militia in front of Bladensburg.

Armstrong followed a little later. He had noted Winder's condition, and he was sure that the President would want him to take over command of the army from the nerve-racked general.

The council had finally been brought to its conclusion when Madison was suddenly confronted by a red-faced man in a Navy officer's uniform who filled the air with seagoing oaths. It was Commodore Joshua Barney, and the tough old salt was blowing his top.

Through the cusswords that flew, Madison was able to learn that General Winder had forgotten all about Barney and his 503 seamen of the Pig Point squadron, and Barney was left without orders.

"Goddammit to hell, sir," Barney roared, "these are the precious few fighting men in the whole damned army."

He explained that General Smith of the District of Columbia militia had refused to give him orders on the ground that he could not, by law, issue commands to a unit from another service. Finally, somebody had offered Barney the job of protecting the Navy Yard.

"By God, sir," Barney shouted at the startled President, "this is thimble-headed stupidity. I am not going to let my five hundred seamen do a job that any damned corporal in the army could do with five private soldiers. I'll harpoon one of these fish-faced officers first."

The idlers chortled and hooted, while Madison stood there seeking to cover his embarassment by touching a handkerchief to his lips. As Barney's torrent lessened, the President turned to Secretary of the Navy Jones and asked if there hadn't been some mistake. The Secretary said there must have been, and hurriedly ordered Commodore Barney to proceed with his men and haul his big naval guns after the army to Bladensburg.

Madison was going to Bladensburg too, and before he left, Secretary of the Treasury Campbell had a gift for him. Campbell was disgusted with the situation, weary of trying to raise money for a war that nobody seemed inclined to fight. He handed the President his brace of big dueling pistols as though turning in his sword. Madison buckled them on; their size seemed to dwarf him and constitute a drag on his movements.

Campbell had used the guns before at Bladensburg when he had outgunned Barent Gardenier in a duel provoked by the latter's charges that the American Congress was a pawn of Napoleon. Now Campbell mounted his horse and rode to his lodgings where he packed his personal belongings and rode off to his home in Tennessee to write his resignation.

Madison, Attorney General Rush and General John Mason were joined by Colonel Decius Wadsworth as they started on horseback for Bladensburg, seven miles away. The President and Rush discussed the possibility of replacing Winder, but as they approached Bladensburg Madison regretfully concluded that he would have to disappoint Armstrong and keep Winder in command.

Madison summoned Armstrong to his side when he reached the army, which was just going into position. He told the Secretary of War he was retaining Winder. "It is too late to make any change," Madison said. "Come with me and leave the decision of the defense to the military authorities, where it belongs."

"You realize this reduces me to the role of a mere spectator of the combat," Armstrong retorted, and angrily stalked away.

Even as Madison arrived on the field, the British Army was approaching Bladensburg from the southeast, on the other side of the Eastern Branch. After a brief slowdown, the troops once more were executing the Moore Quickstep and once again their breath was coming in gasps. There was none of the chatter that marked the American force on the march.

Lieutenant George Robert Gleig was with the advance column under a Major Brown, and his first sight of the Americans came as his column made a turn in the road, circling a plantation a couple of miles from Bladensburg. It was a day of almost perfect visibility, and with his spyglass Gleig was able to get a good look at the Yankees occupying the heights above the town.

The American militia looked most unimpressive. Some of them wore blue uniform coats, but most were dressed in black jackets. Others wore what seemed to be cotton field tunics. To Gleig, as he wrote later, the American Army "seemed country people, who would have been much more appropriately employed in attending to their agricultural occupations than in standing, with muskets in their hands, on the brow of a bare green hill." He did, however, sight some squadrons of cavalry, and on a slight ridge he counted twenty pieces of artillery.

Gleig was struck by the contrast between the two armies, as he looked back and saw his British comrades: "A column of four thousand soldiers, moving in sections of six abreast, and covering an extent of road greater than its windings would permit the eye to take in. . . . The dress, the perfect regularity of their step, the good order which they preserved . . . excited in me feelings for which I have no words."

About this time, an obscure private in the rear rank of the 5th Maryland Regiment also was struck with feelings he found difficult to express. Somehow, John P. Kennedy didn't feel he was dressed quite right for participation in a genuine battle.

Like many of his comrades in the 5th, Kennedy was a dandy. Leaving home a few days before, he had felt assured that the Americans would win a great victory and that, logically, the victory would be followed by a grand ball. Determined to be outfitted as suited a soldier of the 5th, Kennedy stowed into his knapsack a pair of white duck trousers and a pair of patent-leather dancing pumps.

When his regiment had been aroused the night before by the false report that the British were at hand, Kennedy had searched in vain in the darkness and confusion for his marching boots. Feeling slightly silly, he donned his dancing pumps, expecting to recover his boots at dawn. But the regiment was moved to a new position before daylight and Kennedy had to march off without his boots. He now awaited the enemy with his feet cramped and sweating in their fancy ballroom gear.

The Americans set up a great shouting when the British column came into view on Lowndes Heights. But the British marched on silently, "as orderly as people at a funeral," as Gleig remarked.

Shortly an aide-de-camp rode up to Major Brown with orders from General Ross to proceed to Bladensburg, find out if it was occupied and, if so, to dislodge its garrison. Brown's column started off along the Landover road which ran parallel to the East Branch and led to a bridge over the river at the end of Bladensburg's main street.

Bladensburg stood where two roads met and led into Washington—one from Baltimore, the principal highway, and the other from Landover and communities along the Patuxent

River. A few brick houses lined the two streets and the sun glistened on their steeply pitched roofs and was reflected in their dormer windows.

Gleig noted that the road ran for some distance completely under the eyes of the Americans and that it was commanded by several of their guns. But the advance force arrived in the village without hearing a shot fired—and was surprised to find that Bladensburg was deserted.

Gleig couldn't understand this. He remarked to his friend Charlton that a slight rise at the entrance to the town could have been held for many hours by a couple of light field pieces sweeping the road. And he pointed out that the means of retreat across the river was easy and direct.

"I told you the Americans are not very intelligent," Charlton said.

It wasn't all that easy, however. Once in the town, the column had to take to the principal street which lay exposed to the fire of a two-gun battery the Americans had mounted at about the center of their position. As soon as the British showed themselves again, the battery opened fire.

Somebody was serving those guns with a precision rare in the American Army, and the guns were well placed. The first shot dropped three men in Gleig's company, one dead and two severely wounded. At once the column took to the side streets and wound its way in and around the houses until it got out of range, then stopped to rest in the town's center until the remainder of the army could come up.

The main body approached the town swiftly and the two guns opened fire again. But Major Brown had sent a courier back to warn Ross of the danger, and the British force closed up its ranks and dispersed in little units behind the shelter of houses and walls until it could be re-formed for the attack.

It was not entirely safe even behind these shelters. The Yankee cannon kept booming away and Gleig, Charlton and some private soldiers were lying behind a low cottage when there was a crashing explosive sound that lifted Gleig two feet in the air and slammed him against the wall.

The exploding shell had neatly severed the leg of a soldier who had been lying next to the young lieutenant. Gleig kept his control and helped the soldier—and himself—to the only available solace, a tot of rum. Then they waited for the summons to attack.

Across the East Branch the President of the United States was about to witness the battle in which the young lieutenant would take part. Indeed, the mild and erudite President very nearly wandered into the center of the British Army. Leaving his position in the rear, he had ridden through the heart of the American position and was about to cross the East Branch Bridge when an American scout informed him the redcoats were "over there, near Lowndes Hill." Madison turned back to survey the American positions from a safer vantage point.

The battle formation seemed neat and efficient. General Stansbury had placed his artillery in the first line, one battery behind the single trench which commanded the East Branch Bridge and others scattered about. The result was that there was no converging fire on the bridge, an error which later proved fatal. The 5th Baltimore, Stansbury's prize regiment, and two Washington companies were stationed as artillery supports. Pinkney's rifle battalion was just ahead of the guns near the riverbank, and the second line was composed of two other

Maryland regiments. Then, as the British marched into Bladensburg, Colonel William D. Beall arrived with 800 militiamen from Annapolis and they were posted on the right flank, behind the second line.

General Winder and his army had also finally arrived, and Winder arranged a third line on the ridge which followed the District of Columbia line to the southwest, almost a mile behind Stansbury's first line. The battlefield was a gradually rising triangular field, with an orchard and a large tobacco storehouse between the first-line artillery and Stansbury's militia.

The entrenchments hurriedly erected by the citizenry were virtually wasted. Only one unit took advantage of the cover— the field artillery unit which commanded the bridge. The rest of the American Army was out in the open.

Winder certainly was not suffering from overconfidence. In his instructions to Stansbury's artillery he made a most extraordinary suggestion: "When you retreat, take notice that you retreat by the Georgetown road."

There were other contributions equally ill advised. Riding hard from the capital city, there suddenly appeared on the scene the young Washington attorney Francis Scott Key, who within a few months had been converted from a violent opponent of war into a fire-eating zealot determined to bring Perfidious Albion to her knees.

Key's metamorphosis was one of the astounding events of this war, in the opinion of Washington society. Even now, it seemed only yesterday that he had told John Randolph, minority leader of the House: "I will not fight the poor, unoffending Canadians." And when the Americans closed their 1812-1813 winter operations on the Canadian border, Key had written

Randolph further: "The people of Montreal will enjoy their firesides for this, and I trust, many a winter. This, I suppose, is treason, but, as your Patrick Henry said, 'If this be treason, I glory in the name of traitor.' I have never thought of these poor [Canadian] creatures without being reconciled to any disgrace or defeat of our arms."

But Admiral Cockburn's raids in the Chesapeake had changed Key's mind. By late spring of 1814, the verse-writing lawyer had become a lieutenant and quartermaster in Major George Peters' battery, which was assigned by Winder as his principal corps of observation in the Patuxent area. But when Winder decided that the British would be content with "depredations" in the more remote sections of Maryland, he had released the battery from active duty on July 23 and sent its members home. Back in Washington, Key had regaled Washington drawing rooms with his recollection that during his campaigning he was "hit in the face by no more than a piece of salt pork."

Now Key was in the field again, with no official status but burning with the zeal of the civilian sorely concerned lest the military leadership make a botch of things. To the consternation of both officers and men, he rode about the field on a spirited stallion, inspecting Stansbury's line and leading detachments into positions he believed more tactically favorable.

Key shortly was joined by a representative of the estate of politics. This was the wealthy Baltimore merchant, Congressman Alexander McKim, who appeared, mounted on a spirited charger, determined to offer inspiration to the fighting men. Confronted by an officer, McKim declared that since he had voted for the war he was going to stand by and give moral support to the soldiers who were fighting it.

Attorney General Rush even attempted oratory. This young man was an accomplished speaker who had won many votes for Madison with his silver tones during the 1812 campaign. Now he decided the soldiers should be briefed on their glorious duty, and he ranted for five minutes before he was chased away by a sour-visaged officer who thought more of his men's peace of mind than he did of Rush's declamations.

Colonel James Monroe also was on hand. Conscientious and aggressive, he was bombarding Stansbury with ideas for defensive measures. Stansbury listened calmly for a while, then got into a heated argument with General Walter Smith, commander of the District of Columbia militia, over which of them should be second in command to Winder. While they were thus preoccupied Monroe seized the opportunity to ride down to the front line, where he ordered several of the units to shift positions. One regiment he moved from the sheltering apple orchard to a point nearly a quarter of a mile away, where it could offer no significant support to the rest of the first line.

Stansbury was furious when he saw the change. "The order is an outrage and can only result in disaster," he thundered. He also threatened to leave the field, but was placated by Winder.

This was the chaotic scene in the American ranks when at one-thirty o'clock—only ten minutes after General Winder had finally completed the juncture of his two forces—the British attacked.

[X]

"The Rockets' Red Glare"

GENERAL ROSS had been amazed to discover that the bridge still stood over the East Branch, although its destruction should have been the Americans' first order of business. With his light brigade in advance, Ross immediately shot a company forward to force the bridge. At the same time, he ordered his 44th regiment to move north and prepare to ford the stream at its shallowest point.

As the lead company started for the bridge to the clarion blare of the bugles, the British troops were startled to hear a sudden loud shouting from the American forces. It was an exultant shouting, but not because the Yankees were about to tangle with the enemy. Rather, the troops were showing their delight at the news just received that American forces had won a great victory over British General Drummond on the Canadian border. Unfortunately, the report was false.

At first, the Americans operated with considerable efficiency. Pinkney's riflemen, concealed in a belt of woods near the river-bank, rained a hail-like barrage down on the trotting Britishers, and the two-gun battery near the main road to the bridge raked the advance with grape shot.

The British column broke and fell back to the safety of the town, its ranks decimated and its weary troopers gasping for breath. Quickly, the ranks were formed to repulse an American counterattack, but it never came. General Winder was not to turn aggressive at this last minute.

Ross watched through his glasses from a post at the southern end of Bladensburg. An aide standing nearby was fretful lest his general hesitate to pursue the attack.

"What will they say of us in England if we stop now?" he asked.

Ross turned impatiently and addressed the whole little group around him. "Even if it rains militia, we go on," he snapped.

Ross had no artillery, except the two puny three-pounders, to support the crossing, so he stationed some of the light companies of the 85th Regiment behind the willows and larches on the riverbank. He ordered them to pour a constant fire across the river, directed mostly at the wood where Pinkney's riflemen lay in wait. Then he ordered Colonel William Thornton to force a crossing.

Gleig and Charlton were still trying to cosset the soldier whose leg had been shot off, when Thornton rode up to his little advance guard.

"Now, my lads, forward!" Thornton thundered. "You see the enemy—you know how to serve them."

The troops gained the bridge without trouble, but as they thundered onto its plankings, the roadside battery opened up and seven men went down. As the men hesitated, Thornton's hoarse voice could be heard urging "Forward, forward." Forward they went, to be met by the galling fire from Pinkney's riflemen, and more men fell.

This time, however, the British force kept going. The firing from the marksmen of the 85th in the larches on the British side of the stream began to take its toll of Pinkney's men, and they started to withdraw.

The British swept across the bridge, turned quickly to right and left, and threw their heavy haversacks into squad piles along the west bank of the East Branch. Then they formed files of skirmishers ten paces apart and went after Pinkney's riflemen.

Under normal conditions, Pinkney's men might have held their ground. They were well commanded by a distinguished constitutional lawyer who had served his country at the Court of St. James's, and they were confident of their own marksmanship. But now a bizarre touch was added to the situation: Ross fired his Congreve rockets.

The rockets were fired by a special squad which gathered in the fringe of brush along the east bank of the stream, where there was some slight concealment. Hurriedly, the rockets were unpacked from their wooden boxes—long iron tubes laden with a bursting charge controlled by a blaze fuse. The firing cylinders were brought up by seamen, with the tripods that supported them, and shortly the air was filled with these hissing missiles.

Admiral Cockburn was not impressed. "They look damned fine," he told Ross, "but the bloody things couldn't hit the Tower of London at point-blank range."

"It starts furiously, you must admit," Ross replied, "but I vow the thing lands in the most unexpected places. Still, it won't do any harm to us, and it may worry the Yankees."

Even at Havre de Grace the year before, when used without opposition, these rockets had caused only one casualty. They were almost completely unreliable. But to the American troops they were a horrible novelty—a frightening visitation from another world. Ross had calculated rightly when he had estimated their psychological effect on the Yankees, an estimate which had given him comfort when he had originally set out from Benedict.

Pelted by increasing rifle fire, Pinkney's men now found themselves the target of screeching, sputtering projectiles such as they never knew existed. They fell back, and as they did so the British skirmishers pressed forward. Pinkney caught a musket ball in the upper arm, breaking the bone. Some of his soldiers picked him up and carried him with them as they retreated.

Gleig estimated that it took the British only five minutes to clear the little wooded belt of its defenders. "Never did men with arms in their hands make better use of their legs," he later wrote. "Though we did our best to kill a few of them, I question whether one American lost his life in that copse; so rapid, or if you please, so judiciously conducted, was their retreat."

Ross's rockets were now spreading terror among Stansbury's militia in the center of the first line. Ross had ordered their trajectories flattened so they roared toward the American ranks on a nearly horizontal course.

Later, Captain Henry Thompson reported that "not a single rocket struck the American lines." Apparently the range was too long. But the militia was not waiting about for any hits or near-hits. The oncoming missiles, trailing their streams of smoke, terrified the troops; they threw away their muskets and dashed up the hill in frantic retreat.

Colonel Thornton's advance guard had been reinforced by a constant stream of troops from Ross's 85th Regiment and light companies from the 4th and 44th, and this whole force now formed itself into a wide line and advanced to the attack. Meanwhile, the remainder of the 44th had forded the stream on the British right and suddenly came up on the flank of the 5th Baltimore Regiment, commanded by Colonel Samuel Sterett.

The 5th already had had its troubles. When the battle opened, it was in position to Stansbury's rear and slightly to his left. Winder, seeing the center and left of Stansbury's line fleeing from the field, had ordered the 5th to retire—"so you will be put out of reach of the enemy," he told Sterett.

The 5th dutifully retreated up the hill toward Smith's District of Columbia militia—now standing fretfully and gazing with awe at the rockets they believed were bombarding the first line.

There, Sterett found that Winder had decided to countermand the order. "I have an aversion," Winder explained, "to retire before the necessity becomes stronger." So back the 5th went to its original position, reaching it just as the British 44th came up from the river and advanced to the 5th's left flank.

Frantically, Winder ordered another retreat. But the 5th had no more discipline in it after so many confusing commands. Its ranks were unmolested by British fire, but the regiment's morale was crushed. It fell back in wild disorder, many of the men flinging their arms to the ground. Later, Colonel Sterett observed that "We were outflanked and defeated in as short a time as such an operation could be performed."

General Stansbury had done his best to rally his Maryland militia in the center of the first line. Seeing the troops on the right begin to break, he had ridden along the lines ordering the officers to cut down any men who attempted to flee. One company and parts of two others thus were rallied for a few minutes, but when the rest of the force fell back these pitiful few followed them, largely because there was nowhere else to go if they did not want to be outflanked and cut to pieces.

The most serious aspect of this flight of the first line of troops was that they made no attempt to rally when they reached the second line. Instead they fled wildly through the ranks of these fresher soldiers, causing considerable hysteria and hampering the second-line officers in their attempts to form their men efficiently to meet the onrush of the redcoats.

Although less than thirty minutes had elapsed since the first of Ross's troops attacked, a major part of the American Army had deserted the battlefield. General Winder, after the flight of Stansbury's men and the outflanking of the 5th Baltimore, saw no point in continuing to pursue what he believed was a lost cause. Another general with more spirit might have judged differently.

The British had no more than 1,000 men across the river at

that point, and they were still receiving some fire from the right, where Colonel Beall had kept his men in tight order. The District of Columbia militia under General Smith had not yet been within range of the British fire, and its 2,000-odd men—raw though they were—could have been organized into a force capable at least of bloodying the British nose. And although the first-line artillery had been lost, there were still guns ready on the ridge which ran along the District line.

General Smith believed his men wanted to fight. Consulting on the field with General Winder, he told the Marylander, "Damn it, man, the battle hasn't even started for us."

Winder was obstinate, however. He insisted that only further disaster could result from a continued stand. In fairness to him, he had tried to stem the wild retreat of Stansbury's militia and at one point had managed to rally portions of two regiments. But when he left them to return to the 5th Baltimore, whose flank was endangered, the troops became frightened again and resumed their flight, despite vigorous attempts by their officers to force them to stand their ground.

The effect of these fleeing men on the troops to the rear was demoralizing. They began to waver, and Winder pointed this out to Smith in ordering a general retreat. Smith continued to grumble, but even he could see that the troops were already out of fighting control.

There were exceptions to this sad behavior. Colonel Beall, holding a knoll at the right of the third line, south of the Bladensburg-Washington highway, disobeyed the retreat order and kept his men steady. So did Captain Miller, whose Marines were dug in on the roadway in the center of the last American line.

It was at about this time, with the District militia pouring over the countryside in its haste to get back to Washington, that President Madison quit the battlefield, having become the only President ever to be with an American army in battle. He had watched the fighting from a ridge above the third line of defense and when Stansbury's men were routed, he turned calmly to Attorney General Rush and remarked, "I am afraid, sir, that the battle is lost. Perhaps we should return to the capital." Thus saying, they rode off.

Winder was being swept away with his disgraced troops and so was Secretary of War Armstrong. Mounted, Winder arrived at the Capitol ahead of his soldiers, seeking a position where the troops might make a stand. Shortly, he was joined by Armstrong, who sang his old tune: Garrison the Capitol with the retreating troops and use it as a fortress in defense of the city.

While they were discussing this, Colonel Monroe rode up. Apparently he had found nothing useful to do on the battlefield, where most of the commanders had spurned both his advice and his sword. Winder objected to Armstrong's plan, pointing out that there was no way to supply the army with water. Monroe agreed with Winder; he remarked that the militia "showed no inclination to tarry." So Armstrong agreed to a retreat to Georgetown.

Yet the battle was not yet over along that slope before Bladensburg. General Ross at first believed it was when he saw most of the American forces leave the field so soon after the two armies had engaged. Still, he proceeded with caution as he marched his troops up the turnpike toward Washington.

This caution was justified. For the British had still to hear from the only real fighting leader the Americans could boast, Commodore Joshua Barney.

Delayed in leaving the Navy Yard by bureaucratic negligence, Barney and his 503 sailors had been forced to travel slowly because of their burdens. These were five great Navy guns, two 12-pounders and three 18-pounders, drawn by sailors with harnesses about their shoulders. Mules pulled carts loaded with ammunition which Barney had pilfered from Naval stores, much to the consternation of the guards.

Barney was relieved to find there was no one about to supervise his tactics. Quickly, he placed his men and the five guns on a slight rise just over the District line straddling the turnpike up which the British troops were advancing. He was joined by Captain Miller and his 150 Marines, and was pleased to discover that Beall's regiment was holding its ground to his right.

"We'll give 'em a by-God hot reception," Barney told Miller, and Miller grinned in agreement and anticipation.

The enemy made its appearance a few minutes later. The redcoats moved in column on the main highway, with skirmishers in the fields and woods on both sides. They were aiming straight at the center of Barney's position, but when they saw that the hill ahead of them was held by an American force they came to a stop.

But Ross was not going to hesitate long at this point. Quickly he formed his troops for a frontal attack and sent them forward in close order directly up the highway.

As the British neared the beginning of the incline, Beall's militia on the right made their presence felt. A volley of shots rained on the redcoat column. But that was the militia's last contribution to the impending battle. Their muskets still smoking, they broke and ran, heading for the dust clouds that marked

Winder's retreat toward the capital city. Beall shouted and cursed but couldn't hold them.

Worse still, the fleeing men so excited Barney's pack mules that half a dozen of the beasts broke away and dashed after Beall's militia with the reserve ammunition carts. Now Barney and his sailors were all alone on the battlefield with Captain Miller's Marines. The Army would not be represented in the only bit of gallantry displayed that day by an American force.

The British advance consisted of the light troops of the 85th Regiment. Barney ordered one of his 18-pounders to open fire. So accurate was the aim that the gun made a direct hit on the British, blowing an entire company off the road, killing ten men and wounding more than twenty-five others.

Barney squinted ahead at the carnage. "Smite 'em, smite 'em," he kept whispering to himself.

The 85th re-formed quickly and other units of the brigade came up in support. This time the troops began a more general movement along a wider front. Barney promptly brought his other pieces into action and ordered those Marines and sailors not needed to tend the guns to open up with their muskets.

There were no volleys from these seamen and Marines, but instead a continuous, galling fire into the close British ranks. The big Navy guns roared and belched their shells with speed and precision. Twice more the British tried to take the hill by frontal assault, and twice more they were repulsed.

Lieutenant Gleig was with the attackers and he found the musket fire the heaviest he had ever experienced. It seemed to him, too, that the big guns played upon the British without intermission. He felt as though he were in a hailstorm, with the shells of the big guns serving as frequent lightning bolts.

Soon Gleig lost one of his best friends, another subaltern named Williams, who came from a military family and had longed to distinguish himself. Williams was running forward on the edge of a field and had just leaped over a wooden railing when he got it. A musket ball struck him in the neck and he fell dead at Gleig's feet—the bullet having passed through his windpipe.

Ross brought up reinforcements, convinced that he was meeting a new kind of American on that hill. The new troops wore faded red blouses, bleached by the Spanish sun; they were the famous 4th (King's Own) Regiment.

Quickly, Ross widened his lines to the left where there was cover from the woods, and ordered Colonel Thornton to make a new assault. Moving from the woods, Thornton's men advanced against Barney's right—through that glade where Secretary of the Treasury Campbell had dueled and shot Barent Gardenier.

But Barney had anticipated this. He had placed two of his 12-pounders so that they swept the dueling glade, and he now shifted the Marines and all the sailors he could spare to fill the glade with musket balls. Barney waited until the enemy was at close range and then let fly with grape, while the Marines and sailor-riflemen poured lead into the redcoated ranks.

Thornton fell, severely wounded, and great gaps were torn in the advancing line. One musket ball hit Gleig's sword scabbard and another plucked at his sleeve, wounding him slightly in the arm.

Colonel Brooke took command immediately, but before he could re-form the shaken British troops, Barney's men were upon them. A band of wildly shrieking sailors armed with cutlasses and muskets and a line of Marines with fixed bayonets charged down the hill at the startled redcoats.

"Board 'em; board 'em!" yelled the sailors. And the Marines let loose with a terrifying screech—a yell that was to be much favored by the Confederacy during the Civil War.

This was too much for a British force already torn and shattered by those big guns and the amazingly accurate marksmanship of Barney's pickup crew of land fighters. They fled to the cover of the woods. Had Beall's militia stayed on the job, the United States at that point might have forced General Ross to make a full retreat, and thus would have saved Washington from the invader's torch.

The melee had been costly to the Americans too, however. Captain Miller of the Marines was seriously wounded, and of some forty of Barney's men sprawled on the hill, fifteen were dead. Barney's horse had been shot and the Commodore now dashed around on foot, surveying the situation.

What Barney saw was also perceived by General Ross. The American force was too small to protect its flanks. Ross decided that a massive encircling movement would rid him of this obstacle which stood between him and the capital. The King's Own was sent on a wider enveloping movement to Barney's right, and the 85th and portions of the 44th Regiment were ordered to fall on Barney's left and front.

As the British attack converged on the seamen from three sides, Commodore Barney was felled by a bullet in his hip. As he lay behind one of the guns he asked a seaman if there was any sign of reinforcements coming from Winder's troops in the capital. The reply was that if Winder had rallied any of his units they were not returning to the battlefield.

Barney looked up and saw the King's Own wheeling across the high ground in the rear of his right—the ground previously occupied by Beall's regiment. The famed 4th carried fixed bayonets and they were coming fast. The battle was about to draw to a close.

Speaking precisely, Barney ordered his seamen and Marines to withdraw. Three of his men began to improvise a litter to carry him with them, but he stopped them sharply. "I'll stay here where I've fallen," he said. "I'm not afraid of the redcoats."

Some of the men wanted to remain with him, but Barney would have none of that either. His voice became hoarser and his oaths more vigorous as he ordered them on their way.

Gleig was limping painfully in the rear when General Ross and Admiral Cockburn walked up the hill to inspect the position where the Yankees had made their gallant stand. Cockburn's visage wore the look of a man who had been right all along as he surveyed the battlefield and saw the dead and wounded in naval uniforms.

"I told you it was the flotilla men!" he told Ross.

Ross nodded. "Yes, they have given us our only real fighting," he replied.

The British found Barney behind his beloved gun, and Ross and Cockburn went to him at once. They congratulated him on the battle he and his men had put up and gave him his immediate parole.

"Where do you want to be taken?" asked Ross. "To Washington with us, or back to Bladensburg?"

Barney had no desire to see the capital in the hands of the enemy; he said he would prefer Bladensburg. General Ross ordered four men to make a litter and they loaded the commodore aboard for his journey to the hospital. But Barney was irascible.

"By God!" he thundered. "These men carry a wounded man like a sack of corn. Don't you British have any sailors?"

Cockburn grinned and summoned four British seamen to man the litter with the warning that they would answer to him for any discomfort the commodore suffered. Barney shook hands with the red-necked admiral and went off on his stretcher, content at least to be in naval hands once more.

And Ross and Cockburn began laying their plans for the entrance of the British forces into the capital city of the United States.

[XI]

Flight from Washington

LEANING from one of the upper windows of the President's House, Dolly Madison's Negro slave Sukey saw a man galloping up the drive of the mansion shortly before three o'clock on the afternoon of August 24. The man was Jim Smith, Madison's freedman, who had accompanied the President from the Navy Yard to Bladensburg. As he approached the house, he started waving his hat and shouting: "Clear out! Clear out! General Armstrong has ordered a retreat."

Smith was the third messenger from Madison bidding the First Lady take flight. Characteristically, Dolly had ignored the first two, even though her sister, Anna Cutts, had left hours before and had tried to persuade Dolly to go with her.

"Your husband has told you to leave," Anna Cutts told Dolly. "He wants you to leave; he doesn't expect you to stay."

Dolly had been adamant, however, still determined to wait for her husband and be assured of his safety. In the meantime, she had not been idle.

Convinced by the sight of the fleeing soldiery that the Americans were losing the battle whose cannonfire she could hear in the distance, she had sent off to Virginia the several trunks of Cabinet papers she had had stowed in a carriage. Then she had filled a wagon with the silver and other portable articles which were part of the official President's House furnishings, and had directed the driver to haul them to the Bank of Maryland in nearby Montgomery Courthouse. Now, hearing from Jim Smith that the British had swept the battlefield, Dolly Madison decided it was finally time to go. She ordered her carriage brought up from the stables.

This turned out to be a chore. As the capital had descended into anarchic chaos, the city's hoodlums had come out and were running wild. A mob had collected on the grounds of the President's House, and its members swarmed about, looking for something to steal.

The mob confronted Jo Bolin, a slave, as he steered Dolly's coach up the drive from the stables. Bolin had to pull up his horses as the howling delinquents gathered around.

There were cries of "Hang Madison!" and "String up little Jemmy!" Bolin was frightened; the mob clearly intended to take the carriage away from him. He noticed that two of the hoodlums were carrying spades from the mansion's tool shed, and one of them started battering at the carriage door with this weapon.

Bolin was getting ready to jump down from the box and flee when help came. It arrived in the persons of three retreating militiamen, who charged on the mob with fixed bayonets. Most of the mob dispersed, howling. A couple of the ringleaders tried to hold their ground, appealing to the soldiers to join with them.

"Jemmy got you into this," one of the men said. "Why should you protect him?"

One of the militiamen prodded him with his bayonet. "Enough of that," he told him. "Run off with your friends or I'll give you three inches of this blade."

The two men ran, and the three militiamen stood by while Jo Bolin eased the carriage up to the mansion's entrance. "We'll be nearby for a while if you need us," they told the ashen and shaking Bolin. Meanwhile most of the mob had gathered about the coping on the Pennsylvania side to hurl insults at the soldiers.

Inside the mansion, Dolly Madison strode into the dining room. There she caught up as much of the remaining silver and plate as she could stow into her old-fashioned reticule, and then she summoned French John Sioussat.

"John, we must save the picture," she told him.

French John knew which picture she meant because Dolly had told the servants earlier that it must not fall into British hands. It was a portrait of Washington, supposedly executed by the great Gilbert Stuart, and Dolly Madison regarded it as a valuable national heirloom.

Sioussat mounted a short ladder and tried to take down the painting, but he couldn't budge it. He examined the frame. "It's fastened to the wall, ma'am," he told Dolly. "There are screws all around the frame."

"Well, we'll have to chop it down," Dolly told him. "We cannot leave it."

For once, French John—the daring deserter from the French Navy—demurred. "Is there time, ma'am?" he asked Dolly. "I think you should be on your way. Our soldiers have all gone off, like chickens flying from the coop."

Dolly tried to conceal her impatience. "John, there isn't time for *argument*. We must take the painting. Do go and get Magraw and tell him to bring a screwdriver and an ax. If we cannot unscrew the picture we shall chop it away from the frame. It should be quite simple."

French John left to summon Magraw, the gardener. As he left the room, Colonel Charles Carroll walked in—the Charles Carroll whom Madison had left to guard the First Lady and who had unaccountably disappeared a few hours before.

"Why, Colonel Carroll," Dolly greeted him, "I was so worried about you. Are you quite all right? I'm afraid we must leave the President's House."

Colonel Carroll, it appeared, had ridden out to have a look at the battle. Now he was red-faced and sweating—and anxious that Dolly be on her way. "The British will be here at any moment," he told her. "Ma'am, you must leave at once."

"Yes, Colonel, I will," replied Dolly absent-mindedly. "As soon as we get this picture down."

"Picture!" exploded Carroll. "Ma'am, I beg of you. There is no time to bother with a picture."

147

"There is to bother with *this* picture," Dolly said shortly. "Pray, Colonel Carroll, go if you will, but I must save the painting."

So Carroll stood there fuming, as French John returned with Magraw, a hatchet and a screwdriver. Magraw mounted the ladder and tried to loosen the frame from the wall. He got a couple of the screws out, but it was slow going because they were firmly imbedded in the wood.

Carroll was furious. "I pray you, ma'am, we'll be here all evening unscrewing that frame," he told Dolly. "Please, let the man chop away the frame if you insist on saving the picture."

Dolly hated to ruin a fine frame, but there seemed no other way, so she ordered Magraw to wield his hatchet. When he had the painting free from its frame, Dolly intervened again. She cautioned Magraw against rolling up the canvas.

"Lay it on the floor," she said.

Colonel Carroll grumbled that it would be awkward trying to carry the picture that way, and Dolly agreed. But she had an idea. A short time earlier, two men had stopped by the mansion to inquire whether they could be of any assistance to the First Lady. They were Jacob Barker, a Quaker shipowner from New York and a friend of Madison's, and another New Yorker, R. G. L. de Peyster. Dolly had put them to work packing silver. Now she told French John to go and get them. When they arrived, Dolly gave them their historic assignment.

"Gentlemen, we must save this picture," she told them. "Will you take it with you in your carriage at once?"

Barker and de Peyster agreed and carried the painting out of the house. There they found another wagon loaded with valuables, which Magraw was to drive to a farmhouse in Maryland. Barker decided the painting would ride better on top of the wagon load than in his carriage. Whereupon the picture was secured and Barker rode off with Magraw, while de Peyster followed in the carriage.

Dolly Madison still had one other valuable heirloom to save. Striding into the Cabinet Room with a grumbling Colonel Carroll at her heels, she snatched up the embossed copy of the Declaration of Independence which hung on the wall.

"They shan't have this, either," she told Carroll. "The British would be pleased to burn this precious document. This is the original copy, you know."

Dolly was wrong, of course. The original draft, as written by Thomas Jefferson, had been destroyed by the printer Dunlap, after he had set the type and had the proofs corrected. But the embossed document which Dolly saved had all the signatures on it—the latest having been affixed in 1781.

Finally, Dolly Madison told the impatient Carroll she was ready to leave. Her pet macaw had been given to a friend, and the President's House key had been sent by courier to the Russian minister, sequestered in a farmhouse in Bethesda.

"As though that will do any good," Dolly told Carroll. "The British would much prefer to break down the door. But I choose to force them into housebreaking, for the record."

As Dolly got into her carriage with Colonel Carroll and the slave girl Sukey, several members of the mob lurking about the house approached and started hooting at Dolly. "Go and find your husband for us so we can hang him!" one hoodlum yelled.

Dolly paled, and Carroll got out of the carriage, a pistol in each hand, murder in his eye.

"Begone, you damned rascals!" he shouted. "Out of my sight before I shoot you down like the dogs you are!"

The intruders fled, and Carroll got back into the carriage.

"I hate to leave the mansion to those creatures," Dolly told him. "Would that we had a cannon in every window. Then I should stay and help defend my home. But, alas! Those who should have placed them there fled before me."

Then the wife and the inimitable hostess in Dolly asserted itself once again. "Oh dear, my dear husband will never even have a chance to taste it now," Dolly told Carroll.

"Taste it? Taste what?" asked the baffled Carroll.

"The collation, dear Colonel Carroll," Dolly answered. "I had dinner all ready for the President and his associates. It is such a good one too."

It was. Madison had ordered the meal in one of his many messages to Dolly when he was attending the council of war at the Navy Yard just before the Bladensburg battle. He had suggested that he would bring home with him several Cabinet officers and some military men and he urged Dolly to extend her hospitable self since the men were sure to be fatigued and hungry.

Dolly had ordered dinner for the regular hour of three o'clock; this was the hour the President customarily dined, since he rarely ate supper. Jennings, Madison's body slave, had brought up the ale, cider and wine and placed them in coolers. In the kitchen, spits loaded with joints of various kinds turned before the fire, and pots and saucepans of potatoes, vegetables and sauces stood on the fireplace grate. In the state dining room, plate holders stood by the fireplace, filled with dishes. The table was set with fine linens.

Dolly Madison sighed resignedly. "Well, it cannot be helped," she said. "But I do hope my husband will find something to eat elsewhere."

Dolly could find some consolation in the fact that at least some of the would-be dinner guests still observed the amenities. During her vigil in the President's House, the First Lady had received impeccable evidence of this in a note from Mrs. Jones, wife of the Secretary of the Navy.

"My dear Madam," wrote Mrs. Jones. "In the present state of alarm and bustle of preparation for the worst that may happen, I imagine it will be more convenient to dispense with the enjoyment of your hospitality today, and, therefore, pray you to admit this as an excuse for Mr. Jones, Lucy and myself. Mr. Jones is deeply engaged in dispatching the Marines and attending to other public duties. Lucy and I are packing with the possibility of having to leave; but in the event of necessity we know not where to go nor have we any means yet prepared for the conveyance of our effects. I sincerely hope and trust the necessity may be avoided but there appears rather serious cause of apprehension. Our carriage horse is sick and our coachman absent, or I should have called last evening to see your sister. Yours very truly and affectionately, E. Jones."

The First Lady was reminded of this note now, and she confided to Colonel Carroll that "Mrs. Jones was most courteous and ladylike, you know." The baffled colonel quickly banished an impulse to inquire into *that* matter and retreated behind a safe "Yes, umh, of course."

Shortly thereafter, President Madison rode into the city among the retreating troops, resigned to the regrettable necessity of fleeing Washington lest the victorious invaders make a prisoner of the nation's Chief Executive.

Accompanied by Attorney General Rush, Madison went directly to the President's House, where he was relieved to learn that Mrs. Madison already had fled. Then he continued on to the F Street house of Richard Cutts, husband of Dolly Madison's sister Anna. There he drank some cider and ate some bread and cheese, and asked for the loan of a carriage.

The sixty-three-year-old Madison was near collapse and he felt he could not go further on horseback. His exhausting activities of the last few days and the mental torture of witnessing a humiliating American defeat had taken their toll of a frail body already weak from periodic bouts of malaria.

When he went out to mount the carriage, Madison found that somebody had stolen the dueling pistols lent him by Secretary of the Treasury Campbell before the battle. The President had left them in their holsters on the saddle of his winded horse, because he didn't want to carry them into the house with him.

"Oh, well," he told Rush, "I hope I shall not be called upon to fight a duel this afternoon. The day has been busy enough."

In the Cutts carriage, the President of the United States rode on to the Virginia Ferry which carried him into exile on the other side, while Winder's disgraced troops continued to stream through Washington.

The men were dirty, drenched with sweat in the near-100-degree heat, most of them with no weapons. They hurried along Pennsylvania Avenue, where a crowd of dandies had gathered to taunt them with cries like "You're going the wrong way!" and "Oh, see the foot race!"

A few soldiers turned on their tormentors, picking up stones from the dusty street and pelting the idlers with them. One dude had his jaw broken by a haymaker delivered by a Stansbury militiaman. The militiaman celebrated with a long drink from a jug of rum proffered him by one of the painted prostitutes who also lined the route of retreat.

On that dusty afternoon, these husky courtesans were, for once, a credit to their city. They hurried after the retreating troops, giving them water from canteens, stuffing bread in their hands, offering them towels to wipe their sweat-stained faces. Several of the girls went along with the troops, promising their company gratis for the night.

As the troops hurried through Washington they met with some fresh—and irritable—soldiery. These were the five hundred men of Colonel Minor's Virginia militia regiment who had arrived in the capital the day before. But while the battle raged, they had loitered angrily at the arsenal at the foot of Four and a Half Street, Southwest, awaiting the musket flints without which they were powerless.

The troops continued through Georgetown to Tennallytown—headed for Montgomery Courthouse, twenty-two miles from the battlefield. Meanwhile, their baggage had been sent over a different route, across the Potomac Bridge into Virginia, and it was many days before the Army could get them back.

Kindness and encouragement were waiting for them en route. Most of the families which had stayed in their Georgetown houses and in other outlying districts took the men in and fed them. One Mrs. Bradley, whose larder was particularly well stocked, had more than one hundred soldiers in her home at one time, and she managed to dress the wounded as well as provide food for them all.

One of the last of the so-called gentility to leave the capital was Mrs. William Thornton. Once during the afternoon she rode up to the President's House in her carriage but found the door locked and the mansion empty. She went home and had dinner with her husband, who had been busy with a series of errands, and then in the late afternoon they departed for Georgetown, where they stayed with Mrs. Thomas Peters, granddaughter of Mrs. George Washington.

A Mrs. Bates, wife of a militia captain, was left stranded in her home on Seventh Street when both her Negro servants fled. She could not join the flight because her infant son was ill with whooping cough and lay feverish on a trundle bed. In the late afternoon, with the troops filling Pennsylvania Avenue, two hoodlums walked in on Mrs. Bates and demanded money and rum.

Mrs. Bates rose furiously to her own defense. Snatching a long cavalry sword from over the mantel, she swung it with all her strength and chopped two fingers from the hand of the nearest intruder. Shrieking, the pair fled into the street which was now almost deserted.

On the ground of the muddy street, a discarded edition of that morning's *National Intelligencer* reported that "nearly the whole of yesterday passed without any information of importance from our troops or those of the enemy, except a report, for some time believed to be true, that the enemy had retrograded towards Nottingham." Gales had added, with confidence, "We feel assured that the number and bravery of our men will afford complete protection to the city."

The newspaper lay unopened and unread; its readers had fled from Washington.

[XII]

"Burn It, Sir!"

ADMIRAL COCKBURN was anxious to begin the march immediately into the helpless capital of the United States, but General Ross pointed out that there was work to be done. Most urgently, the battlefield had to be tidied up. Moreover, the troops were near exhaustion and they needed an interlude for rest and refreshment.

Squads set to work on the demoralizing chore of collecting the dead. Only sixty-four bodies were found that evening as the dusk settled into darkness, but scores more—reported as missing —had to be assumed dead. Eventually, Ross reported 185 wounded, in addition to the 64 dead, for a total of 249 casualties. But the *National Intelligencer* would later estimate the British killed at 200, while placing the American loss at only 26 killed and 54 wounded.

Lieutenant Gleig may have estimated the British casualties with the greatest accuracy. Limping back to his brigade, a towel tied around his thigh wound, Gleig found that "out of the twelve hundred men who bore the brunt of the battle, nearly one-half had fallen." This would place the casualty total at about 500.

Ross laid out a camp on the Bladensburg field for the major portion of his army, while Cockburn strode about impatiently, anxious for action. The admiral had written Secretary Monroe from Benedict that he planned to "destroy and lay waste such towns as may be found assailable," and he was angry that Ross thus far had not permitted so much as one barn-burning. Cockburn yearned to move on into Washington and set the men to work with ax and torch.

Yet the admiral was nonetheless intrigued by the situation; he penned a report to London noting that the British force was unable to pursue the defeated Americans because "the victors were too weary and the vanquished too swift." Between phrases, he badgered Ross to get started.

Finally, after his men had rested for two hours, Ross formed a new brigade, composed of 1,500 men of the Royal Scots Fusiliers and the 44th Regiment—troops who had seen the least action. The humid twilight was darkening into night as the bugles sounded and General Ross led his men onto the road to Washington.

By eight o'clock, the troops had reached the outskirts of the city and Ross halted his column. He judged it time for a parley with whatever American officials he could find. Therefore, he took a detachment of 200 soldiers and moved forward under a white flag.

Ross was seeking prize money for his expedition. By the customs of war, the American capital was his just spoil and he felt certain that the Yankee authorities would pay a large sum for sparing the city. If they did not, he planned to destroy all military stores and confiscate or burn all records and papers which might be of value to the American war effort.

The general ordered a drum roll and waited with his detachment for a response. But the city was grimly silent under a pallid moon. The streets were empty, the houses dark and shuttered. No one came forward to greet the conqueror.

Moving on with his little force, the rest of the column trailing behind, Ross traversed the Baltimore turnpike and marched down Maryland Avenue. Now he could see the United States Capitol at the end of the avenue—a stark and massive silhouette in the new darkness.

When the British had reached Second Street Northeast, there was a sharp reaction to their entry. Suddenly a volley crashed out from a large house on the northwest corner—the home of Albert Gallatin, who had left his Treasury post to represent America on the peace commission in Europe. The house had been unoccupied since Gallatin's departure the year before.

One British soldier fell dead and three others were wounded.

Another ball killed Ross's horse beneath him and comically undermined the British commander's moment of triumph.

Ross ordered his men to surround the house and shouted at its tenants to come out. When there was no response, he sent a squad of soldiers into the building with orders to shoot on sight. But the house was vacant, and a search of the immediate neighborhood uncovered only a few unarmed Negroes hiding in some bushes.

The house was burned to the ground.

Now Ross led his troops—the smallest force ever to occupy the capital city of a modern major power—into an open field east of the Capitol, a site later to be occupied by the Library of Congress and the Supreme Court. Ross tarried here for half an hour, again seeking contact with American officials so he could discuss an indemnity. But the only persons about were awed Negroes, hovering about the camp with wide and frightened eyes.

Spurring up to Ross's side, Admiral Cockburn held urgent council with the British general. Furious at the attack on Ross's detachment, he demanded that the American capitol building be put to flame.

Ross demurred. His idea was merely to seize and destroy important documents.

Cockburn persisted. "By God, sir, it is but justice," he roared. "Remember, sir, what these Yankees did to York."

Ross remembered, all right. The year before, an irresponsible mob of American militiamen had burned the Parliament buildings of the capital of Upper Canada, an act which had thrown the British public into uproar. Ross knew there was much sentiment for retaliation and, indeed, wondered if it was not his duty to even the score. Still, he delayed a decision, while Cockburn sulked.

"Let us get over there and reconnoiter," Ross said.

Smartly, the detachment of 200 men moved across the weedy field to the Capitol. Standing there in the moonlight, Ross saw two huge wings, constructed of Virginia sandstone, connected by a covered wooden bridge which the young nation hoped to replace with a rotunda and massive dome.

Much of the interior of the building was unfinished; the south, or House, wing had been completed only three years earlier. The new Library of Congress consisted of three rooms above the Senate floor, and the Supreme Court met in the Senate basement.

It was Cockburn who informed Ross of the location of the Supreme Court's quarters, derisively referring to it as "the cellar court." An inveterate gossip, Cockburn had had a horde of Yankee informants reporting to him during his raids in the Chesapeake and they had kept him informed on social chitchat as well as military intelligence. Cockburn now recounted for the preoccupied Ross the story of the day. Dolly Madison and her sister Anna Cutts had descended on the court chamber, hitherto barred to ladies.

"They walked right in like bloody men," reported Cockburn. "Sat there as saucy as you'd please, while the lawyer pleading the case bowed at them." Cockburn neglected to add that later Chief Justice John Marshall had acidly remarked, "The Supreme Court is no place for ladies."

Charging up the steps of the Capitol, Ross's men found the doors barred. Ross was cautious. He ordered a volley fired into the Capitol windows, and the shots echoed through the building with great, metallic bangs. Obviously, however, the Capitol was empty, and Ross ordered his deputy quartermaster, De Lacy Evans, to take a detail and shoot off the locks on the doors.

The doors shattered open, Ross sent a detachment into each of the legislative wings to make certain no Yankee sharpshooters lurked in the nooks or corners. Cockburn stood there on the steps with him, pursuing his pet project.

"Burn it, sir!" Cockburn pleaded. "Blow it up!"

Rose gave the impetuous admiral a tired smile. "Sir, be patient, we probably shall do just that."

Cockburn disappeared and shortly arrived in the chamber of the House of Representatives with a detail of seamen and soldiers, determined to have a little fun. The salty admiral mounted the rostrum and plumped himself in the chair ordinarily occupied by Speaker Henry Clay. He rapped for order with the butt of his pistol.

"Now hear!" roared Cockburn, his red face gleaming in the light shed by a dozen torches. "Now hear! Shall this harbor of Yankee democracy be burned?"

The chamber was split with a chorus of "ayes." Cockburn grinned happily and ruled that the motion had carried unanimously. Then from the corner of his eye he beheld General Ross standing sternly in the doorway. Cockburn strolled casually up to the Army commander.

"Giving the boys a spot of fun," he told the thin-lipped Ross. "My friend, the Prince Regent, will enjoy hearing about it."

Ross said nothing. The scene had offended his sense of discipline; he hated the thought of an officer playing an irresponsible role in front of the men.

"Will we burn it then?" Cockburn asked him.

"Yes," Ross replied. "We'll get onto it at once." It was 9:45 P.M. of August 24.

Ross had been wrestling with his conscience, but he now perceived that, since no American authorities had come forward to ransom the city, it was the British Army's just prerogative to dispose of it as they wished.

Both Ross and Cockburn agreed that the fastest and most efficient method of destruction would be to blow up the Capitol with gunpowder. The British had more powder than they could use, having captured great quantities on the Bladensburg field. But while the two British commanders were discussing the matter, they were approached by some residents of the neighborhood, the first white Americans they had seen.

The delegation pleaded private interests. Members pointed out that an explosion of the force necessary to destroy the Capitol would damage the residences which surrounded Capitol Hill. Ross saw their point after a courteous discussion, and gave orders that the building only be burned.

Once decided on a course, Ross now did the job with characteristic efficiency. He felt that the best place to start the fire was in the wooden bridge between the two wings, and he ordered kegs of gunpowder lodged in the structure. As the powder was set off, dozens of rockets were discharged into the bridge.

The explosion was loud enough to be heard in McLeod's Tavern near the corner of Pennsylvania Avenue and Fifteenth Street, adjacent to the Treasury building. But its force was so carefully calculated that it did no more than shatter a few windows in the houses around the Capitol.

With the bridge burning nicely, the troops now went to work kindling the House and Senate chambers. For tinder, they used books and papers from the Library of Congress, documents found in desks and cabinets in the two chambers, broken furniture, pictures and tar barrels found outside the building.

Among the papers thus consumed by the flames were the last volumes of the manuscript records of the House Committee on Ways and Means, the papers on claims and pensions, and records of claims entered by Revolutionary veterans. Also lost was the "Secret Journal of Congress," and the private accounts and vouchers of Patrick Magruder, clerk of the House.

Fifteen minutes after the explosion, tongues of flame were flicking out of the windows and reaching for the wooden roof, which was covered by sheet iron except for the portion over the Senate wing. Here the old shingle roof had been left on and it caught fire quickly. The wooden floors throughout also fed the blaze, as did the few books left on the shelves of the Library of Congress.

Lieutenant Gleig, watching the fire from his bivouac near the battlefield, found the scene "striking and sublime"; it reminded him of the fiery destruction of San Sebastian during the Spanish campaign the year before.

It was an efficient blaze and within an hour the Capitol had been gutted. The timbers of the Senate wing burned so fiercely that they reduced some of the marble columns to lime. Furniture from other rooms had been piled in the Supreme Court chamber, and when ignited with powder this bonfire caused huge cracks in the columns. The great staircase was blackened and split.

Curiously, two gifts to the young American republic, from the monarch who had aided its fight for independence, escaped the fire. These were portraits of King Louis XVI and Marie Antoinette, which had hung in a room adjacent to the Senate floor. But by the time the troops began gathering tinder for the fire, it was discovered that somebody had cut the canvases from the frames. They were never recovered.

Ross and his troops were about to move on into the center of the city, when another massive fire lit up the sky to the southwest. This was the Navy Yard, put to the torch by its own commandant, Commodore Thomas Tingey, under orders from Secretary of the Navy Jones to destroy the establishment as soon as the British entered the city.

Businessmen and citizens living in the neighborhood pleaded with Tingey to spare the yard, fearing that its destruction would be a death blow to Washington's hopes of becoming a great naval and shipbuilding center, but Tingey had his orders. It was his and Jones's contention that if the Americans failed to fire the yard, the British would do so, and indeed, the next day Ross sent a detail to make certain the destruction was complete.

In addition to Naval stores, ammunition and shipbuilding equipment, the Navy Yard fire consumed a first-line frigate and a sloop of war, many smaller craft, docks, warehouses and machine shops. The ammunition could be heard exploding all night.

The flames lighting up the sky over Washington told the fleeing citizens that the capital city was now in enemy hands. These disheartened refugees saw the fires from various points of vantage.

Madison was jolting along in the Cutts carriage on the Virginia side of the Potomac. Riding alongside were Attorney General Rush and General John Mason, the Commissioner of Prisoners, who had joined the President and Rush at the ferry.

Madison was exhausted, his face gray, his mind in torture.

"Our disgrace is absolute," he told Rush. "We have lost our capital. We must win it back."

Rush nodded abstractedly. "We shall," he replied without conviction.

Dolly Madison was settling down for a restless night in a soldier's tent in Tennallytown, just north of Georgetown. After seeing her safely to the camp, Colonel Carroll had disappeared again, presumably in search of the President, and the First Lady was left with her maid Sukey and the coachman, Jo Bolin.

Sukey thought it beneath the dignity of Dolly Madison to sleep in a tent, but the First Lady cajoled, "See, Sukey, they've put in this nice floor of fresh boards."

"Soldiers' trash everywhere," muttered Sukey, unconvinced.

Secretary of War Armstrong and General Winder were in Tennallytown, too, the former snatching at the lapels of passers-by to deny responsibility for the defeat, the latter brooding in a one-room cottage. Winder had worked for hours trying to lay out a proper military camp for his fugitive army, but the men would not obey their officers, and instead settled down as they pleased in a noisy and chaotic bivouac.

For the British there was still a lot more work to do. Ross ordered an aide-de-camp to get the men moving down Pennsylvania Avenue and into the center of Washington. Cockburn was chuckling happily.

"Forward to the President's Palace," he told the solemn Ross. "I wish I had my new blouse. At last I'll be making my bow in Mistress Madison's drawing room."

[XIII]

A Castle in Flames

THE SWAGGERING Admiral Cockburn was the victim of a transportation emergency as the British troops started their march into the center of Washington. Most of the invaders' horses were spent, and the rest—except for General Ross's new mount—had to be used for patrolling the roads to prevent a surprise attack by American guerrillas. So Cockburn was mounted on a swaybacked mule, the best that could be found in the neighborhood. Somehow, he still managed to look dashing.

"Let us forward!" yelled the admiral. "It's the man that matters, not the beast that carries him."

General Ross led the first of two small British detachments, totaling a little more than two hundred men. The march was a silent one, unattended by drumbeat or bugle call, for Ross regarded it as not so much a triumphal entry as a cautious probing action which might at any moment be assailed by the enemy. Even the soldiers' marching steps were muffled by the thick sandy soil of Pennsylvania Avenue, and their figures were obscured by clouds of dust.

Cockburn led the second detachment, sitting tall on his fractious mule, softly humming a sea chantey. The soldiers behind Ross were solemn of mien, those behind Cockburn were grinning and their step lacked the precision which had been drilled into them. Ross would have given them the rough side of his tongue; Cockburn was too happy to notice their sins against the drill field.

The city was silent. Those citizens who had not fled the capital either kept to their shuttered homes or were sleeping fitfully in huts and cornfields just outside the city. In the woods near Georgetown one woman, who had wandered about for most of the afternoon and night, went berserk and tried to murder a little boy with a hatchet. Militiamen fell upon her and trussed her up. Another woman had marched ten miles from her home near the Capitol to the Maryland woods. Now she was covering her four-year-old boy with a blanket of dead leaves.

It was not until the British column reached Ninth Street Northwest that there was any sign of domestic life in the capital city. Then the British were served notice that not all the inhabitants of Washington felt frightened or defeated.

The agent of this display of America's aggressive spirit was a plump and attractive courtesan named May Willing. For hours she had been sitting in her parlor, watching the American retreat and despondently swigging on a jug of rum. As the British troops approached, May was outraged to see some of her sisters emerge from their houses and lift their petticoats to indicate their willingness to treat with the enemy.

May Willing set patriotism above romance or financial gain. Hurrying to a third-floor window, she laid her hands on every portable object within sight and pelted the British contingent with an assortment of dishes, bric-a-brac—and one heavy chamber pot.

The pot conked a sergeant on the side of the head and felled him like a gored ox. General Ross could see only a vague figure in the window. He had no way of knowing who was thus assailing his force. So he sent a six-man squad to put down the enemy.

May met the detail with feminine defiance. Pressing her attack before the squad could muster their wits, May kicked and scratched and bit her way out of the grasp of two British soldiers before being overwhelmed by the remaining four. Ross ordered her locked in an outhouse and stationed a guard at the door.

The invaders' next encounter with Washington's citizenry occurred in front of Mackgowan's Hotel, also on lower Pennsylvania Avenue, where a small group of residents was gathered to witness the British entry. Ross halted at the hotel and was approached by a Colonel Isaacs. Pointing to the blazing Capitol, the colonel sought to learn Ross's future intentions.

"Will you burn everything, sir?" he inquired. "Even private dwellings?"

Ross was unequivocal in his reassurances. "Sir, you have naught to worry about," he told Colonel Isaacs. "All private property is as safe as though your own troops occupied your city."

Cockburn rode up on his mule to agree. "Sir, you are in the hands of civilized men, not barbarians," growled the admiral. "Pray, calm your fears in the presence of Englishmen."

Then Cockburn spied a copy of the *National Intelligencer*, proffered him by one of the hangers-on. "By God," he told Ross, "here's a droll bit." And he read aloud to the British general a public notice appearing on the editorial page of the renegade journal:

UGLY CLUB

The members of the Ugly Club are requested to attend a special meeting at Ugly Hall, 4 Wall Street, on Monday evening next, at half past 7 o'clock precisely, to take into consideration the propriety of offering to the Committee of Defence the services of their Ugly Carcasses, firm hearts, sturdy bodies, and unblistered hands—His Ugliness being absent, this meeting is called by order of His Homeliness.

Ross smiled despite himself, and Cockburn laughed coarsely.

But Cockburn and Ross found their glee diminished by another item in the *Intelligencer*, headed "Splendid Defence of Fort Erie!" This report told of the repulse of the British at Fort Erie with the loss of 800 men, and had been reprinted from the Buffalo *Gazette* of August 16.

"Damme, it's a lie!" shouted Cockburn. "General Drummond would make mincemeat of those Yankees." But he seemed unconvinced by his own voice.

Ross was too busy with his own immediate problems to mourn over what might have happened to his countrymen at Fort Erie. He wanted to get on with the job, which he now determined would include the destruction of the President's House. As the column moved on, he mentioned this to Cockburn.

"The Yankees burned both Parliament buildings at York," Ross recalled. "I think we should retaliate most vigorously."

Cockburn was delighted. "It will be a good lesson for little Jemmy," he said. "If we don't catch him, at least he'll have to live in a tent."

The British column made its next stop at the corner of Pennsylvania Avenue and Fifteenth Street Northwest, where the avenue turned alongside the small red brick Treasury building. There Ross told the men they could drink at the town pump; he had hitherto ordered discretion throughout the ranks for fear that the Yankees had poisoned other sources of drinking water.

While the men were drinking, Ross and Cockburn entered Mrs. Suter's boardinghouse, south of the Treasury. It was then a little after eleven o'clock and Ross knew that his officers would be hungry when they had done their work. He asked Mrs. Suter to prepare supper for them, explaining that they would be returning later in the evening.

Mrs. Suter demurred. She explained she had only one serving-woman at the time, and suggested that the British party try its luck at the McLeod Tavern, a couple of hundred feet east on the avenue.

"My two sons were in the battle," she told Ross. "I've no heart to be cooking for anyone tonight, especially Englishmen."

Unexpectedly, Ross turned on his charm. He told Mrs. Suter he had heard much about her cooking and the quality of her meats and had been looking forward to the treat of sampling her menu. Mrs. Suter beamed and gave in.

This was probably a lie; Ross's main reason for wanting to eat at Suter's undoubtedly was that the boardinghouse offered a good view of both the President's House and the Treasury and thus he could keep an eye on his men while he ate.

Cockburn, meanwhile, had drifted outside, where he composed a message to Mrs. Madison, promising to escort her to any place of safety she would name. The messenger returned from the President's House with word that the Madisons had fled.

Cockburn chucked a rouged female under the chin. "You see how inhospitable the President and his lady are," he said. "They did not even stay to give us a glass of port."

As the admiral found out shortly, the Madisons had inadvertently extended better hospitality than was at first apparent. The column resumed its march around the Treasury and when the troops entered the President's House they found a delightful surprise awaiting them—the banquet Madison had ordered for himself and other American officials.

The table in the state dining room was set for forty persons, although most of the silver had been carried off by Dolly Madison. The meat on the spits was a little too well done, but it was still warm over the dying fires, and so were the pots of potatoes and vegetables. In the pantry the delighted soldiers found heaps of cakes and tarts.

Cockburn was beside himself with glee. Outside the President's House he had encountered a young American who said his name was Weightman and that he was a librarian. "I'll take you along inside to act as my guide," the admiral had told Weightman, and took him by the arm to emphasize his invitation. Now Cockburn exulted over the banquet spread out in the dining room.

"By God, sir," he told Weightman, "this is a banquet little Jemmy Madison will never taste. But we must be proper guests; I invite you, sir, to drink to your President's health."

Weightman hung back, abashed by Cockburn's coarse geniality. But the admiral snatched a bottle of port from the sideboard, grabbed two wine glasses in his other hand, and motioned Weightman to sit down at the table. Cockburn sat down to pour the wine and then arose.

"To little Jemmy's health!" he roared—and then, to Weightman, "Up, sir, up on your feet!" Weightman stood up, wine glass in shaking hand.

"To little Jemmy's health!" Cockburn repeated. "Damme, sir, drink to your little shrimp of a President!"

Weightman drank. When his glass had been drained, Cockburn slapped him on the back heartily, and the librarian dropped his glass.

Meanwhile, Ross had also helped himself to some port and had signaled his officers to do likewise. "The men may as well eat this food," Ross said. "They must be hungry and it will do them good." Then, almost comically, "I don't think Jemmy and Mrs. Madison will be returning this evening." Cockburn raised an eyebrow at this bit of levity from the solemn Ross.

Some of the men sat down at the state dining table to eat,

while others wandered around in the kitchen, munching on slabs of meat and guzzling ale and cider. Besides beef, there were joints of lamb, squab, roasted and broiled chickens, a wonderfully salty Virginia ham which had to be sliced wafer thin, a great pot of tripe, plates of nuts and apples, and pots of honey to go with the great chunks of bread the men cut for themselves.

Ross cautioned the officers to watch the men closely and make certain they drank none of the brandy and kept away from the newfangled American whiskey. Cockburn already had sampled the Yankee liquor and pronounced it too sweet. Thereafter the crusty admiral stuck to port, which he drank between mouthfuls of squab.

Then Cockburn wandered around on the second floor and reappeared wearing a beaver hat of Madison's which was much too small for him. He told Ross he was looking for souvenirs. Ross regarded him with disapproval, but said nothing.

Motioning young Weightman to follow, Cockburn barged into Dolly Madison's delicate sitting room on the first floor. There he stopped before Dolly's portrait and executed an elaborate bow.

"Most pleased to make your acquaintance, ma'am," said the admiral in mincing tone. "May I compliment you on a most delicious repast. It was most thoughtful of you, milady."

He turned to Weightman. "Young man, make your bow to Her Majesty, Mistress President." Weightman dutifully bent a leg.

Taking Weightman by the arm again, Cockburn strolled into the drawing room. There he was impressed by Dolly's famous draperies with their much discussed fringe.

"Ha!" roared Cockburn. "These will make excellent tinder for our little fire."

He stepped over to one of the windows, ripped the draperies off their fastenings and threw them in the center of the room. "They are much too good for a democratic family, anyway," Cockburn told Weightman. "Damme, but you renegade Englishmen are putting on too many airs." The admiral gestured impatiently at the furnishings around him. "Take something," he told Weightman. "Take yourself a souvenir."

Weightman looked around for the most valuable object in the room, hoping to salvage it for the Madisons. The admiral read his mind.

"No, sir," he said. "Nothing too rich, me hearty." He walked over to a table and picked up a quill pen. "Here, take this. The rest is for the fire."

Cockburn picked up a couple of books, a small picture and a seat cushion from Mrs. Madison's dressing-table chair. He also went through a desk drawer and took from it a roll of papers which Mrs. Madison had stuffed there just before she left. They were the notes in pencil that Madison had sent to his wife from the Bladensburg battlefield. The notes mystified Cockburn, since some of the phrases were inscribed in the President's own system of shorthand, but he took them anyway.

Ross, supervising the men in piling furniture, books and papers in the Oval Drawing Room and other chambers for the fire, was interrupted by a messenger from the French ambassador. M. Serurier had been gazing at the fires blazing in the city and he feared that the situation would lead to mob rule. Respectfully, he asked the British commander to post a guard at Octagon House.

"It's from the French ambassador," Ross told Cockburn.

"Hm, Serurier," said Cockburn. "He landed on both feet. Y'know, he represented Bonaparte too."

Ross sat down at Madison's desk and wrote a reply to Serurier. He told the Frenchman that the "King's Hotel" would be respected as though His Majesty were there in person, that he would give orders to that effect, and that if he was still in Washington the next day he would call on the ambassador.

About midnight the British troops set the President's House afire. They went from room to room with pine torches and poles wound around with great wads of blazing cotton until the flames were visible from every window in the house. Several charges of powder were laid in the basement and set off after the men had left the mansion. Within fifteen minutes the entire building that had been so painstakingly remodeled and redecorated was wrapped in great red flames.

One more destructive blaze remained to be kindled before Ross could adjourn to Mrs. Suter's for supper. Ross ordered the soldiers to fire the Treasury Building, after first sending a detail into the building to collect whatever paper money was to be found and to confiscate the records. The Ross who had hesitated so long before destroying the Capitol now seemed bent on wreaking as much vengeance as he could.

Ross was already at the table, eating, when the front door of Mrs. Suter's flew open and Cockburn rattled into the tavern on his mule, shouting, "Make way for the much-abused Admiral Cockburn." Cockburn tied his mount to a newel post in the hall and sat down grinning. Ross tried not to notice him.

Outside after supper, Ross re-formed his troops for the march

174

back to the camp on Capitol Hill. It was after one o'clock in the morning of August 25, and everybody was tired.

Everybody but Cockburn, that is. The admiral took a detail of soldiers and went back to Mackgowan's Hotel for some more conversation with the Yankee idlers outside. Cockburn wanted to know the address of the *Intelligencer* office and the whereabouts of Editor Joe Gales.

"Gales has been telling some tough stories about me," Cockburn informed the Yankees.

The idlers were close-mouthed, including Bailey, the mail contractor. They said they didn't know where the *Intelligencer* office was located.

Cockburn was furious. "You'll tell me or I'll give you a taste of a British jail!" he roared.

Quickly, two of the men stammered the information that he would find Gales's lair on the south side of Pennsylvania Avenue, between Sixth and Seventh streets. Cockburn hurried there with his detachment.

By this time a tropical shower had descended on the city and everybody and everything was soon thoroughly drenched. Still Cockburn persisted in his mission. He found that the *Intelligencer* office was in a row of buildings which were mostly residences. An officer whom he dispatched to inspect the interior reported that the establishment contained only cases of type, a press and printing materials.

Cockburn expressed his views to the officer. "This is a quasigovernmental establishment," he said. "It prints government propaganda—Gales is a toady of Madison's. We should set it afire immediately."

The officer was not enthusiastic. Aside from Ross's order

protecting private property, his spirits had been subdued by the torrential rain. But the officer did not have to argue with his superior because two American women did it for him.

A Mrs. Stelle and a Mrs. Brush approached Cockburn. They lived in the building adjoining the *Intelligencer* office and they begged him to desist. They pointed out that firing the *Intelligencer* plant would destroy their property too.

Cockburn was his gallant best. "Never fear, ladies, be tranquil," he told them, bowing from the waist. "You are much safer under my administration than you were under Jemmy Madison's." Besides, Cockburn felt the *Intelligencer* business could wait until the morning.

Thus far, as the British column made its way back to its Capitol Hill camp in the small hours of the morning, there had been no casualties on either side. Indeed, except for the fancy lady, May Willing, the Yankees had been most subdued and passably co-operative. But then an incident occurred which resulted in the only death caused by the British entry into Washington.

One John Lewis, a grandnephew of George Washington on Washington's mother's side, had been drinking heavily in a boardinghouse near the Capitol. Lewis was violently anti-British, having been impressed on an English ship earlier in the war. During his forced labor he was convicted of insubordination and condemned to receive five hundred lashes; when the flogging was half finished the skipper had suspended the remaining strokes.

As Ross's leading detachment approached the boardinghouse, Lewis dashed out. A Mrs. Vernon, living in a house next door to the boardinghouse, heard a "clanking of horses" and suddenly a man's hoarse voice saying, "Let's have a pop at him." Seconds later, she was startled to hear the sounds of someone opening her back door and darting down the kitchen stairs to the cellar.

Mrs. Vernon summoned her courage and went into the kitchen. There she saw the trap door to the cellar slowly opening to present the head of an old Irishman named Moriarty, who kept a little shop nearby. He explained falteringly that he had been pumping water outside when he heard a British soldier make the remark about having "a pop at him." Fearful the soldiers were after him, he had dived into the nearest hiding place.

It was, of course, John Lewis whom the British were after. He had brandished a pistol in a sergeant's face, then turned to flee back into the boardinghouse. Five shots rang out and Lewis slumped to the gravel sidewalk, dead, A British soldier kicked the body to make certain it was lifeless; then the column moved on.

General Ross took over some rooms in the home of Dr. James Ewell, who lived in Carroll Row, just east of the Capitol. Mrs. Ewell had fled when the British approached, but was back home when Ross and Cockburn returned to retire for the night.

With rough grace, Cockburn paid his respects to Mrs. Ewell, who still seemed apprehensive. "Why, madam, what could have alarmed you so?" asked Cockburn. "Do you take us for savages?"

Then the admiral noticed several copies of the *National Intelligencer* on a table. "Ay, madam," he said. "I can easily account for your terror. I see from the files in your house that you are fond of reading those papers which delight in making devils of us."

At that moment one of Cockburn's own men was abusing him in language worse than Gales had ever used. When Cockburn had visited the *Intelligencer* office he had stationed a sentry in front of the building to bar any unauthorized entry while the British detail was inspecting the premises. When the admiral departed, he apparently forgot to order the sentry relieved.

And so, for the rest of the night, one lone British soldier—pacing his beat up and down on deserted Pennsylvania Avenue—remained in unmolested and solitary command of the captured capital of the United States.

[XIV]

"Use Your Own Soap"

WHILE DOLLY MADISON was taking fitful naps in her tent in Tennallytown, the President of the United States was spending the night in a house on the Virginia shore of the Potomac, a few miles of woods and one river away.

Jim Smith, who had brought word to Dolly to flee, had also given her a penciled note from the President. It instructed the First Lady to rendezvous with her husband at the farm home of a Mrs. Minor, deep in the Virginia countryside. So on the morning of August 25, Dolly hurried off in her carriage, bound for Virginia.

Dolly and her slave Sukey crossed the Potomac at the Georgetown ferry and drove on into the wooded interior. Both Sukey and the coachman, Jo Bolin, were frightened and unhappy. Curiously, however, they were not afraid of the British troops but of the trashy Americans who were wandering about the neighborhood preying on the refugees.

"Man at de ferry tol' Jo wild men out to get niggers," Sukey confided to Dolly. "They gonna take us and sell us down South to plantation bosses."

Dolly didn't feel too secure herself. She was well aware of the resentment against her husband, and she was sorry now she had refused the military guard offered her at Tennallytown. But she sought to reassure Sukey.

"Sukey, now you just behave," she told her. "There's nobody going to bother you or Jo. We're safe now that we have left the capital city."

Dolly wished *she* could believe it, but she was troubled by the expressions on the faces of some of the men and women whom they passed along the road. They didn't look *friendly*, the First Lady told herself.

From time to time the carriage was stopped so that Dolly could refresh herself at the scattered farmhouses that dotted the area. A Mrs. Love was most kind to the First Lady, urging her to accept her last bottle of cologne after serving her a cup of tea.

Mrs. Madison was not so lucky at her next stop, a tavern crowded with refugees. At first the landlord would not let her in because of the throng which jammed his establishment. But when Mrs. Madison identified herself, he grudgingly allowed that she could go upstairs and wash.

"But use your own soap," he warned after her.

Dolly made her way through the crowd in the common room and tried not to notice the ugly looks and the muttered comments. She hoped Jo Bolin would not be attacked or the carriage taken away.

Upstairs, Dolly squeezed into the grimy bedroom in which were several other women in various stages of undress. The women stared at her and made simpering faces, and one of them —a female with forearms like hams—inquired with mock concern if Dolly had "enough rouge."

Suddenly, Dolly was startled to hear a woman's voice sounding stridently from the hallway. The voice shrieked at "Mrs. Madison" to "come out here."

Dolly walked out into the hall to encounter a tall woman with straggly black hair and a huge, heaving bosom. The woman approached Dolly and wagged a finger in her face. As she did so, Dolly heard one of the other women say in a stage whisper, "It's the landlord's sister."

The tall woman glared at Dolly, her face red and sweating. "Mrs. Madison, if that is you, come down and get out!" she shrieked. "Your husband has got mine out fighting, and damn you, you shan't stay in my house. So get out!"

Dolly stepped back in alarm, and as she did so the woman moved closer and lifted her hand as if to strike her.

From out of nowhere, Sukey hurled herself at the landlord's sister. "You white trash!" screamed Sukey. "You keep your dirty hands off my mistress."

The sudden assault seemed to take the courage out of the

woman. She fell back, looked about her at the other women crowding around, then turned and started down the stairs.

Hurriedly, Dolly Madison picked up her soap—it was too precious to abandon even at such a time and, as Dolly told Sukey, "I shan't leave it for *that* woman." She made her way down the stairs and through the crowded common room, trying to close her ears to the mutterings of the little mob of men and women refugees. Outside, she found Jo Bolin still on the carriage box, chatting amiably with a white boy.

Dolly and her servants continued up Pomitt Run to the Nelson Mill, then through Falls Church. They climbed Minner's Hill and passed by Colonel Beard's place to Buzzardtown, near Langley, in Fairfax County, driving south until they reached Mrs. Minor's estate.

Arrived at her destination, Dolly refused to go into the house until the servants had carried in a trunk she had brought with her in the carriage. She explained to Mrs. Minor that the box contained James Madison's private papers, and asked that it be stowed under her bed.

Mrs. Minor gave Dolly a room of her own—a handsome gesture on that troubled day—and ordered the servants to load all the guns on the place.

"If the British come looking for you, we'll pepper their hides," said Dolly's hostess grimly.

The British were up early. Ross was still eager for further destruction of the capital city, and Cockburn had a few scores of his own to settle. The lusty admiral was up at five o'clock to seek out a better mount than his inelegant mule, and he soon confiscated a small gray brood mare from a stable nearby. Then

Cockburn rode off with a detail of only three soldiers—a small black foal trotting at its mother's heels.

Ross breakfasted with Dr. Ewell, who expressed his regrets that the Library of Congress had been destroyed in the Capitol fire.

"I lament it most sincerely that I was not told of the circumstances that prevailed," Ross said. "Had I known of it in time the books most certainly would have been saved."

"Neither do I suppose, General," said Dr. Ewell, "that you would have burned the President's House had Mrs. Madison remained at home?"

"No, sir," said the general. "I make war neither against letters nor ladies, and I have heard so much in praise of Mrs. Madison that I would rather protect than burn a house which sheltered such an excellent lady."

Ross that morning imposed a curfew and set up a penalty of one hundred lashes for any British soldier convicted of the theft of private property or of damaging any public property without express orders. His order was too late to save from defacement the beautiful monument erected by private subscriptions from Naval officers to their comrades killed in the war with Tripoli.

This monument stood opposite the west front of the Capitol, and the damage to it was discovered by Lieutenant Gleig, whose detachment had moved into the Hill camp that morning. Gleig saw that the pointing finger and thumb of the female figure representing the "Genius of America" had been cut off. Another female figure representing "History" had been robbed of her pen, and the hand had been knocked off the figure of "Fame."

Gleig was shocked by this vandalism, but he was in such good spirits he could not long remain upset. His thigh wound had been newly dressed by a British surgeon established in a house near the Capitol, and he had found a sympathetic friend in the person of a huge Negress who presided over the house.

This ample blackamoor had stuffed Gleig with bacon, ham, eggs and toast, and then presented him with a fresh linen shirt from a bureau drawer upstairs. Gleig felt a momentary sense of guilt when he saw the welcome gift, but the Negress begged him to accept it "for my own sake." He put it on; he had worn his own shirt for more than a week through the long marches, the heat and the drenching storms, and the temptation was too great to overcome.

Gleig did, however, leave his old shirt on the dressing table. Charlton chortled over this. "Her master will never find it," said his brother officer. "It will get up and walk away."

The two British officers took time off to inspect the ruins of the Capitol building. They found that the fire had all but destroyed the interior, leaving just the outside walls and a part of the sheet-iron roof. The wooden bridge which had connected the House and Senate wings was gone, and there wasn't a pane of window glass left.

By now, Ross was marching 900 soldiers—formed in three detachments—into the center of the city to pursue his campaign of destruction. Behind the troops straggled thirty Negroes carrying gunpowder and rockets.

En route, Ross had ordered the torch put to the Bank of Washington on New Jersey Avenue Southeast, near British headquarters. Dr. Ewell had intervened.

"General Ross," he said, "I thought you stated that it was not your intent to destroy private property?"

"Yes," said Ross, "but the Government keeps its money in that bank."

"True," replied Dr. Ewell, "but the building that you intend to destroy is private property; the Government has no bank."

Ross smiled. "You Yankees are persuasive," he told the doctor. "We shall spare the bank."

General Ross found the city quiet but tense. The citizens had learned of a plot by a band of Negroes in Fredericktown, Maryland, to attack the town when the militia was called to the defense of Washington. Eight ringleaders had been arrested and the governor had been asked to call a special court for their trial. The capital's black folk had behaved in a most exemplary fashion, but this news of trouble elsewhere caused new apprehension in a city undefended by its own soldiery and close to anarchy.

Ross sought to allay the fears of a group of residents gathered outside the Treasury Building, which had been only partially destroyed by the fire of the night before. "As long as the British Army is in control here, you will be safe," Ross told them.

The citizens seemed to feel a little better, but their emotions were unsettled almost immediately when Ross ordered his men to set a new fire in the Treasury Building to complete its destruction. The persons of its population might be safe, but Washington's public buildings were not to escape.

Ross's men moved on to the State, War and Navy Building, directly west of the President's House, and kindled another blaze there with their rockets and gunpowder. Ross regarded the ruins of the President's House with satisfaction. Like the

Capitol, it had been gutted and only its outside walls were left standing. The British general wished now he had taken time to save Madison's fine library, but he shrugged off the thought; in time of war, he reminded himself, there is little room for irrelevant courtesies.

But as far as he was able, General Ross did crack down on unofficial looting. When the proprietor of McLeod's Hotel complained to a staff officer that a British soldier had threatened him with his musket and then pillaged several rooms, Ross overheard the discussion and ordered a squad of men to hunt down the thief.

The soldier was found within a half-hour, his tall shako stuffed with silk shawls and pieces of jewelry. He was court-martialed that morning, found guilty and condemned to the firing squad.

With the State, War and Navy Building ablaze, the next stop was an old hotel, formerly owned by Samuel Blodget, on F Street between Eighth and Ninth streets Northwest. The Government had purchased this three-story building, 120 feet long, in 1810 and had renovated it to house the Post Office Department and the Patents Bureau of the State Department. Besides postal equipment, it sheltered hundreds of models of inventions which had been patented by the young nation's creative minds.

Sitting in his Georgetown refuge the night before, Madison's good friend, Chief of Patents Dr. William Thornton, had worried about those very models and felt it was his responsibility to save them. That morning he had risen early and ridden downtown where he had picked up his model maker, a man named Nicholson, the Reverend O. B. Brown and several other citizens. Thornton and his friends were on hand when the British wrecking crew arrived.

Thornton now approached Major Waters, commanding the British arsonists. He told the red-necked Englishman he was about to disobey General Ross's order protecting personal property.

"Personal property?" sputtered the major. "This building, sir, is owned by your Government. It is public property."

"Patents are not the property of the Government, but of the inventors," Thornton insisted. "If you destroy these records of inventive genius you will be committing an act of savagery and vandalism comparable to the burning of the Alexandria library in Egypt."

Major Waters was so confused by Thornton's speech that he was unable to muster a counterargument of his own. He might, for instance, have inquired how Thornton was justified in describing the Post Office Department as private property. Thornton probably would have replied that it was merely a clearinghouse for letters from private citizens to private citizens —at least his wife said as much later.

In any case, Waters was perplexed. He knew Ross as a stern commander who was not the type to permit officers to trifle with his orders. He didn't want to take any chances. "We'll hold off for a while until you see my commanding officer," he told Thornton. "His name is Colonel Jones and he is down the street on the next block."

Thornton raced down the block and confronted Colonel Jones. The colonel demanded Thornton's personal assurance that the patents were personal property. Thornton gave it immediately. Whereupon Jones sent a messenger to Waters telling him to postpone destruction of the building and proceed to Greenleaf's Point to burn the arsenal. Jones's message said Waters could return to Blodget's Hotel later, after someone had gotten General Ross to clarify the issue at point.

The crowd outside Blodget's Hotel missed a famous face; several of the idlers wondered out loud what had become of Admiral Cockburn. "He's busy elsewhere," Major Waters told them shortly. Elsewhere was the office of the *National Intelligencer* where Cockburn had led a detachment to get Editor Joe Gales.

Outside the printing shop, Cockburn told his audience, "I'll punish Madison's man Joe as I have the master, Jemmy." Although Gales's person was safe, since he was with the defeated American troops, the admiral could still vent his rage on the editor's official sanctum.

First, however, the admiral's eye was attracted by a female figure in the crowd. By this time, May Willing had been released by the British on her promise of good behavior. She had spent considerable time on her toilette, and now appeared on Pennsylvania Avenue in the finest party dress she could find. Her face was a tribute to the cosmetic genius of Paris, and she smelled strongly of perfume.

Cockburn sauntered over and May looked him squarely in the eye. "I'll have a kiss, ma'am," he told her, and threw an arm around her waist.

"Not today, sir," replied May Willing equably, and swatted the admiral in the nose with a deft left hook.

Two British soldiers went for her, but Cockburn, his nose throbbing, called them off. "Let her go," he told the soldiers.

"Here is a wench with more spirit than the entire American Army."

Then Cockburn ordered his men to render the *Intelligencer* office *hors de combat*. Gales's library of several hundred books was carted out into the street and burned. His presses were pounded into scrap and his type was scattered in the street. Cockburn threw off the dignity of an officer and joined in the pillage, joyfully upsetting cases of type and helping to throw fresh books on the flame.

The admiral had a specific order concerning the type. "Be sure to destroy all the *C*'s in the box so that the rascals can have no further means of abusing my name," he told his soldiers.

The indefatigable Dr. Thornton arrived just then and decided to intervene again. There was no point in arguing with Cockburn, so Thornton raced to Gales's residence and saved it from destruction by hanging out a sign that read: THIS HOUSE TO LET. Then he went home to midday dinner.

Cockburn's humor seemed so good that some of the crowd dared to exchange banter with him. One of them had a suggestion: "If General Washington had been still alive, Admiral, you would never have got here so easily."

"Sir," replied the admiral graciously, "if General Washington had been President, we would never have thought to come to this fine city."

Meanwhile, Major Waters' detachment had moved on to Greenleaf's Point, a finger of land jutting out into the Potomac southwest of the capital. The nearest American troops were several miles distant and yet, in their efforts to destroy the arsenal, the British suffered more casualties than they did in the opening minutes of the bloody Battle of Bladensburg.

The invader's objective was the destruction of a powder magazine. Most of its contents had been carted away by the Yankees, but a good part had been hidden in an old dry well which had been used as a dump for junked guns and other munitions.

Waters' men prepared the remaining store of munitions for destruction and lit torches to set off the trails of powder leading to the magazine. While doing this, one soldier accidentally dropped his torch into the dry well.

The result was a tremendous explosion. Chunks of earth, stones, bricks and military equipment were blown into the air. Arms and legs were severed and flung in all directions. Three houses were unroofed and the walls of four others were blown in. Windows shattered in houses more than a mile from the blast.

The explosion killed thirty British soldiers and wounded another forty-seven. Most of the wounded were in critical shape, their wounds pitted with powder burns and clogged with bits of clothing, metal slugs and splinters of wood. The injured soldiers were carted to Capitol Hill, where General Ross converted several houses on Carroll Row into a hospital.

Ross's host, Dr. Ewell, offered his services and Ross put him in command of the hospital. Dr. Ewell immediately sent wagons to Georgetown for additional mattresses and dispatched a detail of British soldiers for medicines from a local pharmacist's shop. Ross spent most of the afternoon at the hospital, visiting among the men, and was joined by Admiral Cockburn, who gave Dr. Ewell six gold doubloons to buy food for the patients.

Even before this disaster, Ross had made up his mind to quit Washington and march back to the fleet at Benedict. Always

realistic, Ross knew he could not remain in the capital city in-
definitely without facing an attack by the American troops
which were being re-formed along the countryside. Disturbing
rumors came to Ross's ears that Virginia was mustering 12,000
militia and Maryland had 15,000 more. Furthermore, the British Captain James A. Gordon's squadron, which had been
assigned to sail up the Potomac and capture Alexandria, was
still not in sight.

In addition, conditions in the British camp were frightful—
more dangerous to the men than combat. Bilious fever and
dysentery raged through the camp and scores of soldiers on duty
were suffering from head colds and influenza brought on by days
in the broiling sun followed by nights sleeping in sweat- and
rain-drenched uniforms.

The only tents available were used for the hospitals, and these
were little more than places for men to die in the shade. Traveling light, the British Army had packed few medical supplies, and
the hospital attendants were brutish soldiers good for nothing
else. Frightened of the sick, they wouldn't even venture into the
tents; instead they threw in the daily rations of salt beef, to be
gnawed on by those able to crawl from their blankets to re-
trieve them.

Ross determined to withdraw his men from Washington
that night. But first the British army would be subjected to another frightful experience, this time due to one of Nature's
more violent moods.

[XV]

Retreat—and Return

A SOUTHWEST WIND had been blowing across Washington most of the day. Weatherwise folk knew it portended another storm, and in the British camp on Capitol Hill commissary men hurried to get provisions under cover. Lieutenant George Robert Gleig remarked to his friend Charlton that he hated to get his new shirt drenched by "another Virginia rainstorm."

Gleig underestimated what really lay in store. About four o'clock in the afternoon, the sky suddenly turned black, and in the strange nightlike gloom a terrific tornado struck Washington. Hurricane winds tore whole roofs off houses, blew down brick walls and filled the air with whistling debris. Huge trees toppled, and limbs torn from the few trees that managed to withstand the gale crashed against buildings.

Gleig, who had commandeered a horse, was riding up Pennsylvania Avenue when the storm struck, and the tornado lifted him out of the saddle and carried him ten feet through the air before slamming him against the trunk of a tree. He was all right, but he never saw the horse again. The wind also overturned both of Ross's 3-pounders, which he had planted on Capitol Hill to command the western entry into the city.

The British soldiers huddled in houses and against the walls of buildings, and most of them, unaccustomed to such tremendous violence, were paralyzed with terror. During the height of the two-hour tornado, thirty of the invaders were buried in the ruins of houses which were crumbled by the storm. Two of the thirty died of their injuries.

Ross's plans for withdrawing from the capital had to be suspended for the duration of the storm. Indeed, his colleague Cockburn was marooned in a Pennsylvania Avenue boardinghouse during the blow, and didn't straggle back to camp until well after six o'clock. Cockburn had amused himself, if not the other occupants of the boardinghouse, by parading about in President Madison's hat.

"I kept their minds off the hurricane," Cockburn told Ross when he finally joined him.

When the storm subsided, Ross turned once again to the strategy of withdrawal. He issued a proclamation ordering the citizenry to keep indoors between sunset and sunrise, under penalty of death. Then he called in his officers and informed them that the withdrawal would begin at eight o'clock that night.

The officers, however, were instructed to tell the men to prepare for an important nighttime maneuver connected with the impending appearance of Gordon's fleet in the Potomac. Ross saw to it that this rumor also was circulated by his spies among those Americans still remaining in Washington. Officers' horses were requisitioned to haul the artillery the British had captured from the Yankees at Bladensburg.

Ross felt he had done as much as could be done in the capital. Besides the Government buildings, his men had destroyed two rope walks, the bridge across the Potomac to Virginia, and had captured stores of powder, bullets and provisions. In all, the British had done two million dollars' worth of damage to the capital and left the Congress and the President homeless.

Above all, Ross wanted to avoid another engagement with the American forces. His objective had been attained; there was no point in spilling more blood for no further gain. Whatever might be the result of another battle, he would still have to evacuate Washington, and if he suffered heavy losses he probably would not be able to get away.

Ross ordered that those British wounded who were unable to walk be left in the hospital commanded by Dr. Ewell. He likewise planned to leave the Bladensburg hospital under the command of Commodore Barney. There was not enough time to muster up wagons to carry the wounded all the way to Benedict.

Now huge fires were built all around the camp on Capitol Hill. A few men from each company were assigned to move about the fires so that their figures could be seen by any Americans who might be watching. With the stage thus set, the troops stole to the rear by twos and threes. When they had proceeded far enough to maneuver without being seen, they re-formed into their companies and began their march back to the fleet.

It was nine o'clock on the night of August 25, 1814, when the last pickets quitted the campfires on Capitol Hill. The British troops had occupied the capital city for almost exactly twenty-four hours. Now as they hurried away from Washington, they were reminded of the price that had been exacted for their brief occupation of the city.

The moon rose as they reached the Bladensburg battlefield and an eerie sight confronted Ross's troops. Those dead who had not been buried lay naked on the field, stripped of every stitch of clothing. Their bodies had been bleached by the two storms and their rotting flesh had begun to stink. Human limbs torn off by cannonfire littered the greensward, and muskets and other military equipment were scattered about.

Gleig noticed trails of a white powder on the field and discovered it was flour. The British had confiscated more flour than they could transport, so the soldiers had been permitted to fill their haversacks with it. On the march to Bladensburg, the knapsacks became too heavy for most of the troops and they had dumped out the flour, leaving a trail whereby stragglers were able to make their way to the Bladensburg camp.

At the Bladensburg hospital, Gleig visited a sergeant from his company, who burst into tears when he learned he was to be left behind. Gleig tried to comfort him by pointing out that Colonel Thornton was among those who would fall into American hands. Indeed, he pointed out that Commodore Barney

195

had promised them kind treatment. Out of a mutual respect, Barney had become fast friends with Colonel Thornton during their recent convalescence at the hospital, and he had given Thornton his word. Still, the sergeant kept pleading that he be allowed to limp along with the troops. Gleig finally had to order him to remain where he was.

At about this time, Barney was discovering young John P. Kennedy—the youth who fought in the dancing pumps. Kennedy had suffered two minor wounds and had been carted off with the British wounded.

Kennedy's pumps, set on the floor in all their incongruity, fascinated Barney.

"Did you wear those in the fight?" the Commodore asked Kennedy.

Kennedy tried to grin but managed only a grimace. "Yes, sir, they were all I had," he replied. Then, stammering, he blurted out the story of his lost boots.

Barney rocked the hospital with laughter, then rocked Kennedy with a fatherly thump on the back. "Good for you!" he told the youth. "By God, I'm glad to meet an optimist in this army of rabbits."

Clearly, the old Commodore impressed Kennedy with his naval valor, because the youth would go on to become Secretary of the Navy and to organize the expedition which opened the Empire of Japan to world commerce.

The stay in Bladensburg was brief. Within fifteen minutes Ross had his troops on the road to Upper Marlborough. There he gave the soldiers four hours' sleep before pushing them on again to Nottingham. The British Army arrived in Benedict—

forty miles from Washington—forty-eight hours after leaving the capital.

President James Madison had arrived for his rendezvous with his wife in mid-afternoon of August 25, just in time to escape the tornado which swept over Washington. Dolly met him at the door of Mrs. Minor's hospitable house and threw her arms around the little President.

Until the very moment of her husband's arrival, Dolly had been sure he had been captured by the British. Usually brimming with optimism, she had resisted all Mrs. Minor's efforts to console her. Now she could not resist embracing her husband in public, despite his well-known disapproval of displays of affection.

The Madisons dined that night on wild turkey. A dozen candles lighted their room, while Dolly sparred lightheartedly with Attorney General Rush and General Mason.

"La, sirs," she told them, "it took you long enough to bring my Jemmy to me. I suspect you tarried with a bottle."

Madison looked on, beaming. He was pleased to be reunited with a wife who so often had made him forget the burdens of his office. Sometimes he felt that the strength he had mustered to lead a nation in wartime had come entirely from his buxom Quaker helpmate.

At Dolly's insistence, the Madisons retired early. It was a good thing they did, for after but four hours of sleep they were awakened by a pounding at their door.

It was young Rush with an alarm. A woodsman had reported a British patrol in the neighborhood and the President would have to flee again. Dressing hurriedly, he joined Rush and General Mason, and the three of them were guided through the rain into the fastnesses of the Virginia woods. They spent the night in a woodchopper's hut, while Dolly remained at Mrs. Minor's, sleepless and fearful.

By the next morning, the alarm was discovered to be false, and Madison rejoined his wife at Mrs. Minor's. But they had to part again. Madison wanted to be with his troops who were reorganizing in the Maryland countryside north of Washington. He urged Dolly to continue into the Virginia back country, and he organized a messenger service of neighborhood woodsmen to keep them informed of each other's whereabouts.

When Madison rode away, Dolly made up her mind to do things her way. She considered her ornate carriage a nuisance because it drew attention to herself, and she felt she could do without Sukey and the coachman Jo Bolin.

Her husband had left her in the care of a civilian named Duvall, a forest-wise local planter who was the nephew of a prominent judge appointed by Madison. A local militiaman also had volunteered to help protect the First Lady. Dolly consulted with them: Wouldn't it be better if she disguised herself as a countrywoman before continuing on?

Both agreed with her; Duvall had been privately appalled at escorting the showy carriage into the backwoods, and now he offered to get a horse and wagon to replace it. Mrs. Minor furnished a cotton dress and bonnet and Dolly put them on. Then she summoned Sukey and Jo Bolin and told them it would be their assignment to get the carriage safely back to Washington. The two slaves drove off, trembling.

Dolly departed with Duvall and the soldier in the wagon. Both Duvall and the militiaman were armed but they, too, were dressed in country homespun and, as natives of the area, would have no trouble posing as farmers if they encountered a British patrol. Dolly Madison was rather enjoying herself.

Madison, meanwhile, could find no military men of any authority at Montgomery County Courthouse. He rode on with his companions to Brookville, Maryland, a well-known Quaker settlement, and there found General Winder, about to march toward Baltimore with his militia. Winder reported that the British had evacuated Washington and told the President he feared Baltimore was threatened.

The President let Winder go; he was relieved to discover that the general could do something positive. Secretary of State James Monroe was already on the road with the advance detachment.

General Mason sought shelter for the President in a pretentious home on the main street of the town. The occupant first delivered an abusive lecture on Madison's shortcomings as a leader, then banged the door in Mason's face. Two doors down, the President and his party found refuge in the home of a Quaker, Mrs. Henrietta Bentley.

Also under the Bentley roof was the family of Samuel Harrison Smith, the banker and Commissioner of Revenue for the Treasury. Mrs. Smith wrote that the President was "tranquil as usual, and though much distressed by the dreadful event which had taken place, not dispirited."

In between courses during that evening's meal, Madison wrote letters summoning the Cabinet to a meeting in Washington the following day—Saturday, August 27. Villagers thronged to the Bentley house to catch a glimpse of the President, and several of the more important burghers bustled into the dining room to give Madison the benefit of their views on the situation.

One of these, a physician and a staunch Federalist, seemed pleased at the Americans' defeat. He told the President it was due to Administration bungling. He asked Madison whether now the Administration would continue its policy of maintaining a standing army and navy. Madison was noncommittal. Blustering, the doctor warned the President that a standing army was "an instrument of despotism." Rush and General Mason eased him out of the room.

Madison urged Samuel Harrison Smith to return to Washington as soon as possible. "I shall stay here the night," he told Smith, "and then I shall ride into the capital tomorrow. We shall need all strong hands available."

Next morning, Madison gave a courier the following letter to be delivered to Dolly:

BROOKVILLE

MY DEAREST:

Finding that our army has left Montgomery County C. H., we pushed on to this place, with a view to join it, or proceed to the City, as further information might prescribe. I have just received a line from Col. Monroe saying that the enemy were out of Washington and on the retreat to their ships and advising our immediate return to Washington. We shall accordingly set out thither immediately, you will all of course take the same resolution.

I know not where we are in the first instance to hide our heads but shall look for a place on my arrival. Mr. Rush offers his house in the six buildings and the offer claims attention. Perhaps I may fall in with Mr. Cutts and have the aid of his advice.

I saw Mr. Bradley at Montgomery C. H. who told me that
Mrs. Cutts was well. Jamey will give you some particulars.

Truly yours,

J.M.

Madison reached Washington at five o'clock in the afternoon
on Saturday, August 27, and went with Rush to the latter's
home. That night, Captain Gordon's fleet of two frigates and
several smaller vessels appeared off Fort Washington twelve
miles south of the capital. The garrison immediately blew up
the fort and retreated. Gordon then moved on to the city of
Alexandria where, the next day, he levied a heavy indemnity
which the authorities handed over forthwith to escape the
destruction of their town.

With Gordon's flotilla lying so close to the capital city, Madison changed his mind about Dolly's returning to Washington.
He could not have known, of course, that Gordon planned to
sail several days later to rejoin the British fleet under Admiral
Sir Alexander Cochrane at the mouth of the Potomac without
making any attempt on Washington.

Thus, Madison dispatched another note to his beloved wife:

MY DEAREST:

I cannot yet learn what has been the result. Should the port
have been taken, the British ships with their barges will be able
to throw the city again into alarm, and you may be again com-
pelled to retire from it, which I find would have a disagreeable
effect. Should the ships have failed in their attack, you cannot
return too soon. I shall keep Freeman till the question is decided,
and then lose no time in sending him to you. In the mean time,

it will be best for you to remain in your present quarters. . . .
Inclosed is a letter from Mr. Cutts. My next will be by Free-
man, and as soon as I can decide the points of your coming on.

Ever and most aff'y yours,

J.M.

Dolly apparently did not receive the letter, for in the dark
hours of Sunday morning, August 28, after two days of wandering the Virginia countryside with two men, she reached a ferry
on the Potomac.

The militia officer commanding the ferry refused to take the
three country folk across on his boat. Dolly giggled happily and
identified herself. The officer blushed and, in his confusion,
dropped his hat into the river. Then he insisted on getting a
cushion for the First Lady to sit on during the crossing.

Dolly arrived in Washington shortly after dawn on Sunday.
She went first to the French ambassador's residence, Octagon
House, where the servants routed M. Serurier from his bed to
greet her. Dolly wanted to abandon her wagon and continue
on in the style to which she was accustomed. Would the French
ambassador make her the loan of his carriage? *Mais, certaine-*
ment, but not, please, until he had had the honor of offering
her coffee and *croissants.* Dolly breakfasted, had her hand kissed
several times, and moved on in the ambassadorial coach.

It was a depressing capital city to which she returned. Her
first shock was the President's House, windowless, its walls
blackened by smoke, its interior gutted. Its grounds were littered
with the untidy debris of war—soldiers' helmets, bits of clothing,
beef bones and chicken carcasses, pieces of harness. Dolly looked
once, hard and long, and then looked away.

Along the streets some dead bodies still lay in corners and in doorways, and wounded men cried out from the shanties that sheltered them. Dolly guessed, rightly, that these were the victims of the mobs of looters which had ravaged the city; estimates put forward later would claim that more than fifty persons had been killed or wounded during the lawless depredations that followed the retreat of the American forces.

By the time Dolly reached the capital, the indefatigable Dr. William Thornton had invoked his authority as a justice of the peace to assume control of the city. With the aid of friends and neighbors, he had put a stop to the looting, but there was little he could do to allay the people's fears that seamen from Gordon's flotilla soon would be roaming the city's streets.

Indeed, as Dolly was riding on to the Cutts home on F Street, Madison was conferring with Thornton and others at the Thornton house, next door to the Cutts residence. Mrs. Thornton lent the President a spyglass and he mounted to the fourth floor, to search the horizon over the Potomac. When he came downstairs, Dr. Thornton sought to brief him on the attitude of the people.

"I have been canvassing the city," Thornton told Madison, "and the people are violently irritated at the thought of our attempting any more futile resistance."

Madison was displeased with this intelligence, and so were Attorney General Rush and Secretary of State Monroe; the latter had arrived in Washington several hours before the President.

"There will be no armistice deputations," Monroe told Thornton, and the President nodded. "It is up to the people to arm themselves and defend their capital."

Mrs. Thornton, busy nearby, could not restrain a sniff of disdain. Later she told a neighbor that "It sounded very bold to say they would not surrender, after we were conquered and the public property laid to ruins." She was disturbed, too, when Dr. Thornton went upstairs for his sword and left with the President's party "to join the people and to call on them to arm."

About that time, Mrs. Thornton looked out her parlor window and saw Mrs. Madison arriving at the Cutts home, in what she later described as a "parroty" carriage; apparently she meant gaily painted.

Madison was out about the city when the First Lady arrived at her sister's, and the First Lady took advantage of his absence to change clothes and freshen her appearance. When the President arrived with Monroe and Rush, he and Dolly greeted each other most casually, considering that the First Lady had been "lost" for two days.

They embraced, of course—Dolly would not overlook that feminine ritual, but then they launched immediately into a discussion of the probable intentions of Gordon's fleet. As the wife of the President, Dolly always put first things first and she could not let herself indulge in affectionate phrases celebrating the reunion when the capital appeared to be in danger once again.

The President immediately busied himself with preparations to defend the city against a possible second attack. Despite the defeatist attitude of the people, he ordered defensive works built on a low hill near the southeast waterfront known as Windmill Hill, and General Smith's District of Columbia militia was summoned back to the city to man the defense.

Mrs. Thornton was efficiently busy too, on matters concerned with sickroom hygiene. By this time, her husband had discovered that there was a British officer named William Thornton in the hospital in Bladensburg and the doctor somehow had found time to pay his namesake a long, chatty visit. He had returned with a list of necessaries he wanted to bring to the British officer and had left it to Mrs. Thornton to round them up.

"A bedpan!" Mrs. Thornton commented aloud as she went over the list with Mrs. Smith. "We used to have two, but some rascally nigger ran off with one of them." She pondered the problem for a while, index finger to nose, then got up and reached for her bag. "I'll borrow one," she told Mrs. Smith. "I'll just go up and down the street until I find one." She was back ten minutes later, triumphantly brandishing the bedpan. It was delivered to Colonel Thornton that night.

Meanwhile, Secretary of War Armstrong had emerged from his hiding-place in the woods and returned to the capital. He kept away from the Capitol, where someone had sketched on the charred walls the figure of a man hanging from a gallows, with the inscription: "Armstrong the Traitor." But shortly thereafter he rode over to Windmill Hill to exercise his authority.

Armstrong's arrival threw the camp into complete confusion. One of the first persons he encountered was the wealthy Charles Carroll. Armstrong offered his hand to the proprietor of Bellevue, and Carroll refused it. Then Carroll launched into a loud denunciation of Armstrong's conduct, causing such a scene that General Smith hurried over to see what was the matter.

By the time Smith arrived, the whole camp was in a commotion. Carroll had shouted that he would not serve under Armstrong. Now several officers of the militia approached Gen-

eral Smith and offered him their swords. A spokesman put it
to Smith bluntly: "There, sir, are our swords. We will not
employ them if General Armstrong is to command us in his
capacity of Secretary of War, but we will obey the orders of
any other member of the Cabinet."

General Smith realized that feeling against Armstrong had
gone too far for successful conciliation. He sent two aides to
report to the President, who was found riding down F Street.
Madison made his decision on the spot. He told the aides to
report back that no orders would be given by Armstrong which
conflicted with those the President had already issued.

Clearly, Armstrong's sun had set. Yet the President tried to
handle the matter gently. He summoned the Secretary of War
and suggested that he leave Washington until public indignation
had waned. Armstrong rode off to Baltimore, where he signed
his resignation and sent it to Madison.

As might have been expected, James Monroe immediately
stepped into the vacuum. Without even consulting the President,
Monroe assumed the duties and authorities of the War portfolio
which he had held for several weeks the year before. Madison
decided to observe what he would do, and for the time being
to say nothing about Monroe's unauthorized command.

The President could not stand aside for long. Bustling about
the defensive works in front of Georgetown, Monroe ordered
a colonel to change the positions of some guns. The colonel
pointed out in ripe language that Monroe had no authority to
issue such orders. Monroe replied that the colonel could either
obey the orders or leave the field. Huffily, the colonel walked off.

Friends of the colonel brought the case to Madison's attention.
The President realized that he no longer could equivocate.

Monroe was one of the few first-class leaders the Government could boast, and his military competence was an established fact. Madison appointed Monroe Secretary of War.

At the same time, Madison dispatched a courier with a message to Governor Tompkins of New York, offering him the post of Secretary of State. The President felt he had to compensate that important state for the loss of important Cabinet representation. When Tompkins declined the appointment, Monroe remained Secretary of State as well as Secretary of War.

[XVI]

"Is the Flag Still There?"

HISTORY SEEMS TO HAVE a penchant for whimsey. In the midst of the great events happening in and around Washington, D.C., during that late summer of 1814, two minor incidents combined to set the stage for the casual birth of a proud and confident national anthem.

The incidents were unheroic and, in a sense, anticlimactic. They involved some British stragglers and an arrest by the redcoated invaders of an American physician of hitherto questionable loyalty. But combined they would eventually cause a Washington attorney to compose a song called "The Star-Spangled Banner."

The stragglers were the last straw to a Maryland countryside sick of the annoyances and inconveniences of war. General Ross's retreat to Benedict was so swift and fatiguing that it left these stragglers panting behind, traveling singly or in little bands. Freed from military discipline, they looted farms and roadside houses of food and liquor, and terrorized the womenfolk.

Maryland was outraged by these depredations. Among the most indignant Americans was Dr. William Beanes, whose farm had been British headquarters during Ross's stay in Upper Marlborough, and who had extended such gracious hospitality to the invading troops. Dr. Beanes visited with his neighbors and inveighed against the pillagers; the Americans, he said, should rise up against them.

Former Governor Robert Bowie, who had considerable property in the area, felt the same way. He clattered into Upper Marlborough on one of his blooded stallions and conferred with Dr. Beanes. Shortly they organized a band of vigilantes sworn to rid the neighborhood of these military grifters. The protests of certain residents who feared British retaliation were dismissed as cowardice.

The same day—Friday, August 26—Bowie, Beanes and one John Rodgers led a posse which arrested six British soldiers and escorted them to the Queen Anne jail. Soon scores of citizens showed up at the jail to hurl insults at the prisoners and promise them dire punishment.

Unfortunately, a seventh British soldier got away. He raced

off to try to catch up with the main column and en route encountered a troop of British cavalry, sent back to discourage possible American pursuit. The straggler told his story of the six arrests, and the wheels of British retribution were set in motion.

At one o'clock on the morning of August 27, a detachment of British cavalry suddenly appeared at Dr. Beanes's home. They arrested Dr. Beanes and also two house guests, Dr. William Hill and Philip Weems, neither of whom had taken part in the capture of the six stragglers.

It was a rough night for the sixty-five-year-old Dr. Beanes. He was snatched from his bed and permitted to put on only a pair of trousers over his nightgown before being lifted onto the bare back of a farm horse. Dr. Hill and Weems were given similar mounts. Then the detachment and their prisoners rode through the night and most of the next day, until they reached the British fleet at Benedict.

Before departing, the British had delivered an ultimatum to the residents of Upper Marlborough: Unless the British prisoners were released by noon, the invaders would return and burn the town to the ground. Promptly, the jail doors were opened for the stragglers.

Bowie heard of the incident at his farm three miles outside of town, and took to the saddle. He rode after the British troops to the Benedict camp to intercede for his friends. The British locked him up, too, and a detail of cavalry was sent to strip Bowie's farm of its food.

A petition from the residents of Upper Marlborough for the release of the prisoners won freedom for Hill and Weems; General Ross interrogated them personally and was satisfied they had not participated in the vigilante project. Somehow, Bowie also persuaded his captors to release him, although the arrest of the stragglers had been largely his idea.

But Ross refused to release Beanes. Possibly he was annoyed that a man who had seemed sympathetic to the British cause had turned on his former guests. At any rate, he stowed Beanes away on one of the ships and indicated that the doctor would be transported either to Bermuda or Halifax to stand trial for treason. The charge was justified, in British eyes, because Beanes had been born in Scotland.

Beanes's friends were alarmed; treason could be punished by death. A petition from Prince Georges County residents was ignored by Ross and Cockburn, and the situation began to look hopeless. Now a planter named Richard E. West took a hand in behalf of his family physician. West was a brother-in-law of Francis Scott Key, the Washington attorney who, for his own amusement, sometimes jotted down bits of verse. He rode to Georgetown and asked Key to intercede for Beanes.

Key agreed and went to President Madison. The President accredited Key as a governmental emissary to the British commander, and sent him to consult with General John Mason, the American commissioner of prisoners. Mason gave Key a letter to John S. Skinner, a Baltimore attorney who was Mason's agent in negotiating exchange of prisoners.

Key had been fired with patriotic zeal ever since the British marched on Washington. He was also a clever lawyer who realized that he would need psychological assistance if he were to deal successfully with Ross and Cockburn. He wanted to be able to argue that the release of Beanes would be to England's own self-interest.

Leaving Washington on the night of September 2, Key made two stops before riding on. The first was at the hospital on Capitol Hill, where Dr. Ewell was working eighteen hours a day attending the British soldiers who had been wounded in the explosion at Greenleaf's Point. The second stop was at the hospital in Bladensburg.

The canny Key made it known at both hospitals that he was bound for the British fleet and would be glad to carry any letters the patients might have. He filled two saddlebags with these messages for loved ones in England, and in all of them soldiers mentioned that they were receiving excellent treatment at the hands of their captors. One Sergeant Hutchinson even gave Key a similar letter addressed to General Ross himself.

Key detoured to Baltimore to pick up Skinner, who told him he had written to Ross reminding the British commander of the rules of civilized warfare. Beanes, Skinner wrote, was an unarmed noncombatant, and his arrest violated "the known usages" of armies in the field.

From Madison on down, American officials were really much more interested in preserving a policy than simply in the release of Beanes. They feared that Beanes's arrest might set a precedent that would disturb the recently executed exchange agreement. If the British were permitted to make prisoners of civilians, they would do so whenever they needed a few more captives to effect an equal exchange with the Americans. Beanes was a symbol of the nation's determination to protect its civilian citizenry from military harassment and its captive soldiers from unjustified detention by a sly foe.

Aboard the exchange boat *Minden*, Key and Skinner spent two days looking for the British fleet. They found it on September 7, lying at anchor near the mouth of the Potomac, and went aboard the *Tonnant* to confer with Ross and Cockburn.

The two British commanders were cordial but coy. They were not interested in even discussing the Beanes case. Cockburn in particular grew incensed over what he called the "preposterous suggestion" that the doctor be freed.

"That old man will get no compassion from me," roared Cockburn. "We'll take him to Halifax and try him and then hang him."

Ross was soft-spoken but firm. He told Key Beanes had violated his noncombatant status "by laying hands on a British soldier." Both Ross and Cockburn refused even to let Key see Dr. Beanes, and would not let him send the prisoner the package of soap and clothing he had brought with him.

Then Key produced the letter from Sergeant Hutchinson. Ross read it solemnly, then skimmed through several of the letters written by other British prisoners. General Ross was not a man who had to be hit over the head with a hint. He understood what was at stake and quickly arrived at a decision.

Ross's decision was the only one that could have been expected from a man so conscious of his responsibility to his men. The British commander would not jeopardize the wounded he had left behind him.

"Dr. Beanes will be released," Ross told Key. "He deserves more punishment than he has received. But I feel myself bound to make a return for the kindness which has been shown to my wounded officers—and upon that ground, and that only, I release him."

Cockburn was disgusted. He strode from the cabin, kicking at the furniture as he went. Ross sat down and wrote a letter to

General Mason. Beanes would be released, he told Mason, "not from any opinion of his not being justifiably detained, nor from any favorable sentiment of his merit, but purely in proof of the obligation which I feel for the attention with which the wounded have been treated."

But it was a week before any of tne Americans would be permitted to leave the ship. Ross explained that the fleet would be sailing into the Patapsco River to move on Baltimore and he would take no chances of the Yankees revealing the British plans.

On the night of September 13, 1814, Key, Skinner and Beanes were on the *Minden* when the British fleet began its bombardment of Fort McHenry, which guarded the water approach to Baltimore. They remained on deck all night, anxiously watching the American flag which waved over the fort and which was lighted from time to time by the British rockets.

It was a big flag—thirty-six feet long by twenty-nine feet wide—but Dr. Beanes complained he had difficulty in seeing it because of the smoke of battle. As dawn slipped onto the scene on the morning of September 14, Beanes kept asking Key: "Is the flag still there?"

Key had become irritable and his repeated "Yes, Doctor, it is" began to take on a snappish quality. Yet the scene, and the repeated question, "Is the flag still there?" made a peculiarly vivid impression on Key's emotions. It seemed a fine thing to be an American and to be witnessing the repulse of a British fleet by an American fort flying the emblem of a free nation. From time to time he scrawled a few notes on a scrap of paper.

Key felt even better later that morning when the bombardment ceased and he and his fellow Americans were released. En route to dry land, he kept muttering phrases, occasionally matching them with a tune that kept running through his head.

"The Star-Spangled Banner" was composed by Key that night in a Baltimore tavern. The music he lifted from a British drinking song, "Anacreon in Heaven"—the tune that had been dancing through his head on the exchange boat. Its composer, John Stafford Smith, had written the song for the Anacreonitic Society of London. Skinner listened unimpressed as Key sang the anthem.

"It's too high," the exchange agent told Key. "People can't sing a song like that."

"But they'll listen to it," Key told him.

And the next day the Washington attorney took the poem to his brother-in-law, Judge J. H. Nicholson. The judge liked it and accompanied Key to the office of the Baltimore *American,* where a printer's devil named Samuel Sands set it in type. The anthem first was issued as a handbill entitled "Bombardment of Fort McHenry," and it first was published in the Baltimore *Patriot* of September 20, 1814. But Congress would not adopt it as the official national anthem until March 3, 1931.

[XVII]

The Phoenix Rises Again

THE BRITISH INVASION was sputtering to a tragic end. About
the time when Admiral Cochrane was starting to fire his first
shells at Fort McHenry, General Ross's forces landed at North
Point, fourteen miles from Baltimore. Ross wanted to take
Baltimore as his winter headquarters, from which he could
emerge for frequent punitive expeditions while Cochrane's
fleet guarded him on the water.

On the morning of September 14, Ross and Cockburn had

breakfast at a farmhouse near the shore, eating well on fresh eggs, milk and chickens. After breakfast, the pair prepared to depart and Ross stopped to thank the farmer.

"Will you be back for supper?" asked the farmer.

"No, sir," replied Ross with unaccustomed force. "I'll have supper in Baltimore." Then he paused and added, "Or in Hell."

As the army formed for the march, Ross called his aide, Duncan McDougall, and the two took up positions with the advance party. Soon the two of them were riding ahead to a clump of oak trees, where Ross stopped to survey the country with his spyglass.

An American rifle corps was concealed in some brush below the low hill on which Ross stood. Two shots rang out, and Ross fell back into McDougall's arms. He called his wife's name once, and died.

British soldiers, pushing on, saw Ross's body on the ground under the oak trees and mourned, tears streaming down many faces.

In the battle that followed, both men who had fired on Ross were killed—Daniel Wells and Henry McComas.

But the campaign ended in failure. When the fleet failed to take Fort McHenry, the army was forced to retreat—a circumstance which considerably strengthened the hand of the American peace commissioners then negotiating with the British at Ghent.

Later Parliament honored Ross with a monument in St. Paul's, and the Prince Regent raised him posthumously to the peerage, proclaiming his family Ross of Bladensburg. Ross's colleague Cockburn went on to capture Martinique, birthplace of the Empress Josephine, and to command the ship which transported Napoleon to his exile on St. Helena.

There Cockburn, characteristically, dismissed Napoleon, declaring that "on the score of talent, he is just an ordinary fellow," and Napoleon replied with considerably greater insight, "Cockburn is not a man of a bad heart; on the contrary, I believe him to be capable of a generous action. But he is rough, overbearing, vain, choleric and capricious."

In the city made desolate by the torches of Ross and Cockburn, James Madison now led a staunch little band of patriots who were no longer fighting a war, but fighting to keep the fourteen-year-old capital from becoming a ghost town of ruins.

Outside of Washington, especially in New York and New England, the presumption now was that the capital would be moved to another location. After all, the Federal city had been virtually destroyed, and Washington had never been a popular capital anyway. Its summer weather was atrocious and winter turned its dirt streets into avenues of mud.

Along with its condolences, Philadelphia sent an emissary with an invitation to move the government back to its old quarters on Chestnut Street, and offered a house, free, for the Madisons. New York City gave the Government its choice of several handsome buildings.

President Madison's actions were those of a man unaware that anyone had even proposed such a move. He summoned Congress to a special session on September 19, and ordered Dr. Thornton to move his patent models from Blodget's Hotel so the building could be refurbished to accommodate the legislators. Dr. Thornton had already put a crew to work repairing the roof of the building, which had been damaged by the tornado.

In this respect, Dr. Thornton was more confident than his wife. She wrote her sister, "God only knows when the executive government will again be organized." And Mrs. Samuel Harrison Smith was writing, "It is not to be expected that Washington will ever again be the seat of government."

But Washington was insistent upon its survival. Within a few days after the British withdrawal, the banks had reopened, and the *National Intelligencer* was publishing again—thanks to equipment borrowed from an assortment of Baltimore printers. Madison told a critic, "Of course we shall carry on here on the banks of the Potomac, where the will of the people has placed the capital."

From Monticello, the erudite Thomas Jefferson forwarded an intellectual offering. He desired to present the nation with his excellent library, which had taken him forty years to accumulate. Eventually, a grateful Congress paid $50,000 for his books, and they were transported to Washington in a wagon train by a contractor paid five dollars a day for the trip. Jefferson's library more than compensated for the few volumes lost in the burning of the infant Library of Congress.

Jefferson also managed to squelch a project which many believed would be a left-handed tribute to the British invaders of the capital. As plans for the rebuilding of the Capitol progressed it was proposed to erect a plaque on one wall to commemorate its burning. Jefferson argued that such a tablet would please Britons more than it would inspire Americans; the project was abandoned.

Meanwhile, public support of Madison's stubborn determination to keep the Government in Washington was bolstered by the departure of Gordon's flotilla from Alexandria. After raiding that city of most of its provisions, Gordon did some desultory cannonading of the capital's outskirts, but shortly received word from Cockburn to catch up with the main fleet.

"We have done all that was possible in Washington," Cockburn wrote Gordon. "It would not be sensible to waste cannonballs on a city reduced to ashes."

Besides, Ross had counseled against any attempt at another landing. Gordon could spare less than one thousand men for such a project, and Ross believed the fired-up Americans could handle such a force and, by a minor victory, salve the Yankees' wounded pride.

Following Gordon's retirement, Madison called for volunteers to help rebuild Fort Washington, and hundreds of citizens responded. With work on the entrenchments well under way, the workers one day noticed an old man in homespun, vigorously wielding a spade. One of the officers found the old man's face familiar and stopped to chat with him.

It was Major Pierre Charles L'Enfant, the French engineer whom George Washington had commissioned to lay out the capital city. L'Enfant had disappeared into obscurity after being relieved of his duties for refusing to permit publication of his plans. Now he had returned, as he put it, "to help rebuild the city I conceived."

L'Enfant could take solace from the fact that his wide avenues and system of traffic circles designed for defense had never been put to the test. Washington had fallen because its defenders had not tried to defend it.

Unlike L'Enfant, the rest of the nation at first reacted to

the burning of Washington with anger and vitriolic criticism of Madison and his Administration. In New York, the *Spectator* expressed its rage.

"Yes, Fellow-Citizens, we have to record the humiliating, disgraceful fact that, in the third year of the war, the City of Washington, the SEAT OF OUR GOVERNMENT, situated 300 miles from the ocean, and in the very heart of this great and extensive country, has been captured and its public buildings destroyed, by a paltry force of 5,000 men."

And the *Evening Post* posed a list of rhetorical questions:

"Is it possible that after being two years at war, our capital, the seat of our general government, should have been left so defenseless? Can it be believed that a small armament of a few ships, and from six to ten thousand troops, which came into our waters on the 17th instant, could demolish our capital on the 24th?

"Were there no means of defending the property of the nation? Can men who manage in this way be fit to govern a great and free people?"

But after this first wave of anger the nation settled down to face the facts of life. The Washington disaster might have been Madison's fault, but that was already history. Overnight, the nation united in its determination to pursue this unpopular war with new vigor, to take its revenge on a power which had shamed an independent people by burning its capital.

Throughout the country, the people flocked to Madison's support. The Governor of Vermont, a state which had been highly vocal in its opposition to the war, suddenly proclaimed that "the war has assumed an entirely different character," and had become "a common, not a party, concern." Volunteers gathered in New York to work on the construction of Fort Green on Brooklyn Heights. New York State announced a loan of $1,000,000 at seven per cent to finance its war effort since, as the *Post* explained, "the National Treasury is empty." Promptly, the Federalist Rufus King announced: "I will subscribe to the amount of my entire fortune."

The *Post* was caught up in the patriotic fervor. "But one sentiment should animate us," its editor declared. "Shall we basely surrender our country, or nobly and honorably rise in our might and crush the foe that has polluted the sacred soil of our birth or our adoption?"

It was the same almost everywhere. In Newark, New Jersey, 1,000 citizens marched out to work on the waterfront entrenchments, each man wearing on his hat a card carrying Captain Lawrence's famous words as he lay fatally wounded on the deck of the *Chesapeake:* DON'T GIVE UP THE SHIP! Philadelphia's City Council borrowed $300,000 for defense, and private business pledged another $1,000,000. Baltimore embarked on a project to arm fifty small vessels and send them to attack the coastal trade around the British Isles. Two hundred women helped with the fortifications at Charleston, South Carolina. Boston began the erection of a new fort in its harbor.

Washington Irving, whose prose now brightened the pages of *Salmagundi* magazine, furnished a stirring example of this new sentiment. En route to Albany on a Hudson River steamboat, Irving heard a passenger comment on the burning of Washington, "Well, I wonder what Jemmy Madison will say now?"

Irving turned on the man and swung from the heels, catching him on the side of the head with a hefty right. The man went down heavily, and Irving picked him up again before the man even knew what had hit him. Irving sat the man down again, and held his lapels while he delivered a lecture—in the precise and formalized language of that literary man:

"Sir, do you seize on such a disaster only for a sneer? Let me tell you, it is not now a question about Jemmy Madison or Johnny Armstrong. The pride and honor of this nation are wounded. The country is insulted and disgraced by this barbarous success, and every loyal citizen should feel the ignominy and be eager to avenge it."

Thus relieved of his feelings, Irving proceeded on to Albany and offered his services to Governor Tompkins. The governor appointed him his aide, with the rank of colonel.

By the time Congress assembled, on September 19, in Blodget's Hotel, public opinion was pretty much in favor of keeping the capital in Washington. But those politicians in favor of moving were not surrendering lightly. Some of the lawmakers seized on the inadequacy of Blodget's Hotel as a telling reason why Washington should be abandoned.

"In regard to ourselves," said Representative Stockton of New Jersey, "here we are in the Patent Office, in a room not large enough to furnish a seat for each member when all are present, although every spot, up to the fireplace and windows, is occupied."

Jonathan Fisk of New York introduced the resolution for removal of the seat of government, and the debate was on again. Jefferson came to town to observe the proceedings and Monroe confided to him that "We have the votes; there'll be an avalanche of talk, but we shall win out."

Still, the debate was long and furious in the House. New Yorkers and Philadelphians saw their chance to kidnap the capital and their voices roared on in cogent argument. It was not until October 15 that the move to abandon Washington was defeated by the narrow margin of 83 to 74. Madison, Monroe and Jefferson literally talked the legislators into it.

"Some day the nation will thank you on bended knee," Monroe told Madison.

Madison smiled wryly. "Not those who happen to be in the city on a sticky July day," he replied.

Madison also had seen to it that other government departments established themselves swiftly in temporary quarters, so that Washington could have the appearance, at least, of a working capital.

By September 9, the State Department was operating in the house lately occupied by Judge Duvall; Treasury was in the former home of the British Minister; the War office in a building adjoining the Bank of the Metropolis; the Navy office in Mr. Mechlin's house near the West Market, and the General Post Office in what the *National Intelligencer* described as "one of Mr. Way's new houses."

Now Washington's citizenry named a committee of seven to direct the job of preserving and rebuilding the city. The first chore was to provide a meeting place for Congress, since it was clear that Blodget's was an inadequate makeshift. A wealthy landowner named John Law took the main initiative.

Law was an Englishman who had struck it rich in India, where he was associated with Lord Cornwallis. He had served under General Winder in the latter's paltry defensive efforts, and since then had been roundly condemning Winder for his poltroonery. People listened to a man who owned five hundred lots in the capital city, and they responded with cash when he announced a public subscription to build a home for the Congress.

Law's efforts included the personal recruitment of carpenters and bricklayers. So impressed were these workmen by his enthusiasm and energy that they fell to and constructed a long, brick building on Capitol Hill in 102 days. The building would become known as the "Little Capitol," and later, as the "Old Capitol." John C. Calhoun lived and died there, and during the Civil War it was a military prison which housed, among others, the Lincoln conspirator, Mrs. Surratt. Subsequently, it was also occupied by the Woman's National Party before being razed to provide space for the new Supreme Court building.

During the early stages of this frenzied rebuilding activity, the President of the United States was forced to live with his in-laws, Mr. and Mrs. Richard Cutts, in their F Street house. Madison didn't mind. He spent most of his time in town during those busy days, and at night he was too weary to notice his surroundings.

The only thing that troubled the President was the detachment of fifty militiamen assigned to guard the Cutts house. He felt it was ostentatious and unnecessary. But James Monroe insisted on maintaining the guard. From her home next door, Mrs. William Thornton worried about the men sleeping on straw in the rain, and thought the President and Dolly Madison were becoming quite heartless.

Her husband objected to the President's continued residence

next door too, but for a different reason. He felt the nation's pride and dignity required that a suitable home be found for the Chief Executive.

Soon, then, the busy Dr. Thornton called at O'Neill's Hotel to visit with Benjamin Tayloe, who was indisposed. The good doctor inquired about Tayloe's ailment, and then came to the point. Would Tayloe lease his home to the Government for the use of the President and First Lady?

Tayloe was a staunch Federalist who thoroughly disapproved of Madison. But now everybody was standing together. Besides, Thornton had designed and built Tayloe's Octagon House, now occupied by the French ambassador, and Tayloe and Thornton were associates in the breeding of race horses. Tayloe put his name to the dotted line a few days later.

Moving in a short time later, Dolly Madison was fascinated with the house. It was not so much octagonal as it was partly triangular and partly circular, and it had a great deal of distinction. For one thing, it was built of brick instead of the sandstone popular at the time, and it had curving doors, window sashes and even curving window glass. An innovation were the two small iron stoves in the wall of the vestibule, which warmed winter guests on arrival.

The President took over as his office a circular chamber above the vestibule. Dolly Madison began to plan a series of receptions in the great drawing room on the main floor, with its long, unbroken floor boards and elegant chandelier.

At about this time, British newspapers started to make their appearance in New York and Washington, and Americans were surprised to discover that the burning of Washington was looked on with indignation in some journalistic quarters in "perfidious Albion." Editorial voices were raised in protest against what was called a British lapse into barbaric warfare.

"Willingly," said the London *Statesman*, "would we throw a veil of oblivion over our transactions at Washington. The Cossacks spared Paris, but we spared not the capital of America."

The Liverpool *Mercury* warned that the fires in Washington would ignite the American soul: "We will content ourselves by asking the most earnest friends of the conflagratory system, What purpose will be served by the flames of the Senate House at Washington? If the people of the United States retain any portion of that spirit with which they successfully contended for their independence, the effect of those flames will not easily be extinguished."

One British newspaper, however, treated the matter with contempt: "There will be great joy in the United States on account of the destruction of all their public and national records, as the people may now invent a fabulous origin. They will, however, find a sore obstacle in the *Newgate Chronicle*."

The *Chronicle*, of course, was the calendar listing biographical information on the notorious murderers, highwaymen and thieves who had been tenants of Newgate prison, many of whom had emigrated to America.

All over the world the burning aroused unfavorable reactions. Dolly Madison's son Payne, with the peace commission in Ghent, first learned of the burning of the capital a month after it happened. Eventually, on October 9, 1814, Payne got around to writing Madison about it. Addressing his stepfather as "Dear Papa," Payne wrote:

"About ten days ago we received the painful news of the destruction of the public buildings in Washington. This act of the enemy meets with universal excoriation and has induced for the first time the Paris Journals to publish what was supposed contrary to the inclinations of the British Government. I must also regret my absence, for if I could have been serviceable in no other way I might have been perhaps useful to my mother.

"I send by this opportunity some newspapers and an article in manuscript as a specimen of one of the late essays which appeared in the Paris Journals. I have reason to believe it and probably some others to have been written by Mme. de Stael, who requests me to make known to you her high respect."

From Octagon House, James Madison rode out daily to watch the rebuilding of the capital city. Even in the dark depression that had seized him with Washington's occupation, he found cheer and inspiration in the sight of workmen going about the brisk motions of restoring Jefferson's dream city to its former rather untidy glory.

Benjamin Latrobe had been called back to his architect's desk to supervise the rebuilding of the Capitol, and the Irishman James Hoban, who had designed the President's House, was commissioned to restore the executive mansion. "The British have burned and pillaged," noted the *National Intelligencer*, "but posterity is assured of enjoying a determined nation's restoration of these shrines."

Both Latrobe and Hoban were determined to renew "these shrines" according to the original plans. But at the President's House, Hoban had to deviate slightly from the plans to re-create what had been. The fire-resistant stone walls still stood, but they were so blackened by the flames that they could not be restored to their original pristine beauty. There was nothing to do but paint them, and thus produce an effect which would give the nation a new name for the home of its Presidents—the White House.

[XVIII]

"Is It Peace?"

THERE HAD BEEN rejoicing in the United States, particularly in the restive North, when, early in 1813, Czar Alexander of Russia had offered to mediate between the American and British governments. Madison had promptly accepted the offer and dispatched to St. Petersburg Albert Gallatin and James Asheton Bayard, who joined John Quincy Adams, the American minister to the Czarist court, in a hopeful commission of peace.

Bayard was a man of forty-five who had distinguished himself as an eminent lawyer and legislator. He had served three terms in the House and one term and part of another in the Senate. He was a Federalist who had opposed the war before its start but who had given it his full support once the fighting began.

Great Britain was not so eager as Madison was to secure Russian mediation. The Foreign Office believed it could deal with the Americans once Napoleon was disposed of, and refused to enter the negotiations, claiming it did not want to deal with a third power. Thus for more than a year the American commissioners drifted about Europe, including the enemy city of London, where, after Napoleon's fall, they took part in the celebration and learned of new moves against their country.

Still, the Prince Regent kept the door open. He suggested the peace delegation meet in London or Gothenburg, Sweden, believing that while new arrangements were being made, the British forces would have time to administer a series of decisive defeats to the Americans. Taking the Prince Regent at his word, Madison added two new members to the commission—Henry Clay and Jonathan Russell.

Madison had sent for Clay and had bluntly told the Kentuckian, "You have driven me into this war; what can you do to help me out of it?"

Clay had been reluctant at first to join the peace commission, but agreed because Madison insisted it was his duty. Madison told him to be aggressive and to imply that America was planning a new and more vigorous campaign in the field.

"Don't be too stubborn, however," the President warned him. "Enter into the best arrangement you can."

But even after Clay and Russell, the American minister to Sweden, had arrived in Europe, the Prince Regent continued his delaying tactics. He wanted news of British victories to bolster his position. It was not until August 6, 1814, that the peace delegation finally got together in Ghent, which both sides had agreed upon as a substitute for Gothenburg. The sessions began two days later.

A deadlock occurred almost immediately. The Americans wanted the treaty to deal with impressments, the rights of neutrals and blockades. The British wanted to talk about an Indian buffer state running from Sandusky, Ohio, to Kaskaskia, Illinois, British control of the Great Lakes, the cession of most of Maine, and the dismantling of American forts on the Canadian border.

Clay was furious. "We may as well go home," he told Adams. "I knew this would happen."

But Adams persisted. He asked the British to put their demands in writing, and when they complied, he sat up all night to compose a reply that was a masterpiece of logic. In London, the Prince Regent sent his commission new instructions—to continue the negotiations by seeming more conciliatory.

Meanwhile Adams was having his personal troubles with the American peace commission. None of the other members liked him, and Clay in particular took delight in jarring the ascetic New Englander, who rose every morning at five, with his own conduct, which was liberal and relaxed. His behavior apparently had its desired effect.

Adams wrote in his diary: "I dined again at a table d'hôte at one. The other gentlemen dined together at four. They sit after dinner and drink bad wine and smoke cigars, which neither suits my habits nor my health, and absorbs time which I cannot spare. I find it impossible, even with the most rigorous economy of time, to do half the writing that I ought.

"Just before rising, I heard Mr. Clay's company retiring from his chamber. I had left them . . . at cards. They parted as I was about to rise."

Clay joked about Adams. "We should find him a nice young filly," he told Gallatin, who was shocked. Adams heard about it and considered writing Madison asking for Clay's recall. But events intervened.

The British commission sent word to Adams that they desired to renew the talks. There was considerable haggling, but by mid-October the British had capitulated to the extent of a proposal that each country retain permanently such territory as it might hold when the war ended. The Americans, who had dropped the impressment issue, plumped for *status ante bellum* —the conditions existing before the war.

In some quarters, Britons believed the Americans were about to give the British commission a trimming. The London *Times* was among those who felt the delegation in Ghent should be warned about getting too soft. It declared: "The fancied conquerors of Canada will be mighty glad to come on their knees and cry, *pœnitet, miserere nostrum!* but we hope their hypocritical lamentations will not be considered by our Ministers as a reason for excusing them from one iota of the amends they ought to pay. Low and humble and penitent as the scoundrels now appear for their offenses, they will shortly revenge themselves by a double portion of audacity and insolence."

233

News came from America, but it was not the news the Prince Regent had anticipated. Instead of British victories, there had been defeats at Plattsburg, Baltimore and on the Canadian border. The news outraged a British public already sick of the war and weary of high taxes. The Cabinet had to decide whether to make peace or spend another ten million pounds to despatch more troops to Canada.

Wellington was summoned and asked to take command in Canada. The Iron Duke's reply was startling. He said he was, of course, always subject to orders, but that he didn't believe anyone could succeed in North America. "The need there is control of the lakes, not more soldiers or another general," Wellington told the ministers. "I do not believe there is an urgent reason why we should demand any cession of territory by the United States."

Politicians did not openly disagree with Wellington. His opinions carried enormous weight with the British public. So, in Ghent, the British commissioners asked the Americans to submit the draft of a treaty.

The treaty ultimately agreed upon was a victory for neither side. The two nations had fought to a draw in a war that had been unpopular on both sides. The war had been a consequence of the war between England and France, and America's position as a neutral. With France and England at peace, the United States had no neutral position to protect, and there were no longer any impressments or blockades. There was no mention of impressment in the treaty, because the American delegation felt this threat no longer existed. Similarly, the British conspiracy with the Indians in the South and West had collapsed, so the treaty ignored that issue too.

Clay had opposed recognition of the Treaty of 1783, which gave the British the right to free navigation of the Mississippi River. Adams, however, was unwilling to risk having the British renounce a similar agreement which gave the Americans rights in the fisheries off Labrador and Newfoundland. In the end, both sides agreed not to mention either of these privileges, on the theory that if a dispute arose later it could be handled independently.

To be sure, the treaty was expedient. But British reaction was that the Americans had fared much better. The London *Times* published an imaginary "Advertisement Extraordinary," purportedly from the hand of the public printer:

WANTED—*The spirit that animated the conduct of Elizabeth, Oliver and William.*

LOST—*All idea of national Dignity and Honour.*

FOUND—*That any insignificant State may insult that which used to call herself Mistress of the Waves.*

"The war, to speak tenderly of it, has not been a very glorious one," said the *Times*. And it went on to suggest that the nations of continental Europe will "reflect that we have attempted to force our principles on Americans and have failed. Nay, that we have retired from combat with the stripes yet bleeding on our backs. To make a peace at such a moment, they will think, betrays a deadness to the feelings of honour and shows a humility of disposition inviting further insult."

Nevertheless, upon the signing of the peace documents the delegates from both sides prepared a gala party to celebrate

235

the occasion. In that connection, the leader of the band engaged for the celebration approached the American delegation with a request for the music and words to the young nation's national anthem.

The delegates chewed this over for more than half an
hour; some of them insisted it was "Hail, Columbia!" while
others held out for "Yankee Doodle." Finally "Yankee
Doodle" was decided on, but the band leader discovered that
no one in the delegation knew the tune. The New Englander,
Adams, confessed rather shamefacedly that he never even
whistled that sectional air.

Clay summoned his Negro valet, John. "John," he told
him, "whistle 'Yankee Doodle' for this gentleman."

And as John whistled the tune, the band leader took it down
in pencil, and the next evening the band played "Yankee
Doodle" with such verve that it brought down the house.

"Not a very inspiring tune," Gallatin whispered to a
Britisher, "but somehow fitting as a droll dirge for this ridiculous war." Both sides then agreed that it had been a very
pointless war.

Now one more piece of incongruity was to be added to it.
The Treaty of Ghent was signed on December 24, 1814, and on
December 26, Henry Carroll, one of the secretaries of the
American delegation, started for Washington with a copy of the
treaty. He went first to England, where he boarded the British
sloop of war *Favorite*, and sailed from Plymouth on January 2,
1815. And on January 8, 1815, with Carroll on the high seas
and America still unaware that a treaty had been signed, General
Andrew Jackson decisively defeated a British expeditionary
force at the Battle of New Orleans.

Because the battle was fought after the treaty of peace was signed, some historians later would dismiss Jackson's victory as indecisive. Actually, however, the United States and Great Britain were not at peace at the time. The Treaty of Ghent was merely a recommendation; it would not become binding until ratified by Parliament and the Prince Regent, and by President Madison and the Senate.

In the meantime, the British commander at New Orleans had sweeping orders: to gain control of the mouth of the Mississippi River and to take territory that Great Britain might then claim under the keep-what-you-have principle. Had the British forces under Major General Sir Edward Pakenham won the battle, there is little doubt that England would have laid claim to the whole lower Mississippi Valley and to most of the Southwest.

At Octagon House, therefore, President Madison was despondent as he awaited news from New Orleans. He had had too many unfortunate experiences with American military leadership to pin much faith in Jackson, and he was depressed by what seemed a stalemate in the negotiations at Ghent.

Even on social occasions, the President's depression was evident. It was noted at a large dinner at Octagon House on January 21 by a young Bostonian named George Ticknor, who had arrived with a letter of introduction from John Adams.

Ticknor wrote his father: "The President, too, appeared not to know all his guests, even by name. For some time there was silence, or very few words. The President and Mrs. Madison made one or two commonplace remarks to me and others.

"After a few moments a servant came in and whispered to

Mr. Madison, who went out, followed by his Secretary. It was mentioned about the room that the Southern mail had arrived, and a rather unseemly anxiety was expressed about the fate of New Orleans, of whose imminent danger we heard last night. The President soon returned, with added gravity, and said that there was no news! Silence ensued.

"No man seemed to know what to say at such a crisis, and, I suppose, from the fear of saying what might not be acceptable, said nothing at all."

Actually, the defeated British had evacuated their entrenchments at Villeres' plantation two days before—on January 19. The news of the American victory finally reached Octagon House a few days after the dinner which young Ticknor had found so depressing.

In her diary, Mrs. Samuel Smith spoke for most Americans: "We are all rejoicing over the good news from New Orleans. Oh, if we had had a Jackson, we should not have exhibited such a shameful sight." And the Postmaster of New Orleans, Thomas B. Johnson, wrote Dolly Madison that "The country is saved, the enemy vanquished . . . all is exultation and jubilee."

Henry Carroll arrived in New York on Saturday, February 11; the *Favorite* had been thirty-eight days in crossing the Atlantic. Landing at the Battery at eight o'clock in the evening, Carroll went to the City Hotel on Broadway near Center Street and casually mentioned to the manager that he was carrying a peace treaty to President Madison.

Within twenty minutes, Broadway was lighted up by hundreds of men and women carrying lighted candles and shouting "Peace!" Taverns were crowded with the celebrators, and one publican set a keg of beer out in the street so that the poorer folk might toast the good news without charge.

At noon on Sunday, Carroll left for Washington in a post chaise drawn by four horses. Twelve hours later he passed through Philadelphia, where he delivered the good news. He did not arrive in Washington until just after dark Tuesday evening, February 14, but somehow his news had preceded him. Rumors had reached the capital city Monday night, by express from Baltimore; the people tried hard to believe them.

The post chaise, lumbering through Bladensburg in the new dark of Tuesday evening, now followed the same route Ross and Cockburn had taken when they entered and burned the city the previous August. The night was clear and cold, but Pennsylvania Avenue was a mudhole, since it had been raining for more than a week. Horses and post chaise, therefore, were covered with mud when the coach drew up in front of the home of Secretary of State James Monroe.

A crowd of men and boys gathered outside and cheered while Carroll presented himself to Monroe and accepted a tot of rum. Then the two men went down the street together to deliver the treaty to President Madison.

Madison was sitting in the large drawing room with the First Lady and Dr. and Mrs. William Thornton. They were talking of peace, more hopeful now that Jackson had saved New Orleans. When Monroe and Carroll were announced by French John Sioussat, Dolly jumped out of her chair, but the President rose slowly and walked over to greet his guests.

"Is it peace?" he asked Monroe.

"Yes, it is peace," Monroe replied. "Mr. Carroll has the treaty here."

Carroll handed the copy of the treaty to Madison, and the President sat down at a table and began reading it. But Dolly Madison could not contain her joy; she ran out into the big circular hall and cupped her hands to her mouth.

"Peace!" she shouted. "Peace! Oh, rejoice!"

Jim Smith appeared at the top of the basement stairs. Dolly called him to her side.

"Serve wine to everybody," she told him. "Take care of all the servants. Let them have all they want."

The capital city of the United States was drunk for two days.

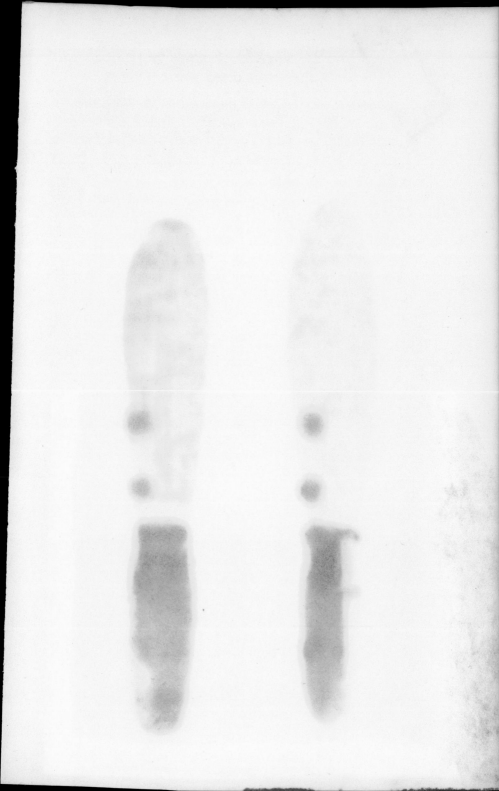

4/25/61

42732   E
                                            356
                                            W3
                                            T8

TULLY, ANDREW
    WHEN THEY BURNED THE
WHITE HOUSE.

DATE DUE

Fernald Library
Colby-Sawyer College
New London, New Hampshire

GAYLORD   PRINTED IN U.S.A.